MAKE YOUR OWN
LAMPSHADES

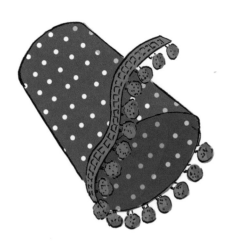

MAKE YOUR OWN
LAMPSHADES

35 original shades to make for
table lamps, ceiling lights, and more

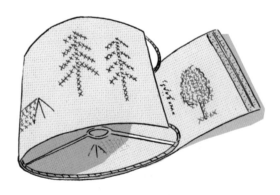

Elizabeth Cake

CICO BOOKS
LONDON NEW YORK

Published in 2013 by CICO Books
An imprint of Ryland Peters & Small Ltd
20–21 Jockey's Fields
London WC1R 4BW

519 Broadway, 5th Floor
New York NY 10012

www.cicobooks.com

10 9 8 7 6 5 4 3 2 1

A CIP catalog record for this book is
available from the Library of Congress
and the British Library.

ISBN 978-1-78249-045-6

Printed in China

Editor: Clare Sayer
Design: Isobel Gillan
Photography: Emma Mitchell, Gavin
Kingcome
Styling: Sophie Martell
Illustration: Michael Hill

NOTE: All projects provide
measurements in both metric and
imperial. Please use only one set
when cutting out and sewing, as they
are not interchangeable.

Contents

Hello!

A few years ago, after searching for a lampshade that was a bit out of the ordinary to hang in my apartment—and coming home empty handed, again—I decided to teach myself how to make my own. I consulted my collection of vintage craft books, adapting the old patterns and instructions for the twenty-first century, and eventually set up Midnight Bell in 2010, making drum and bell-shaped lampshades from reclaimed metal frames and vintage fabrics. I have been teaching others how to do the same in workshops across the UK ever since.

It's easy and fun to make lampshades tailored to your own décor, requirements, and taste, so there's no reason for the lighting in your home to be dictated by whatever happens to be in the shops. You could make something to coordinate with your soft furnishings or wallpaper but I recommend getting really creative, to produce beautiful, colorful, eye-catching one-off pieces that make you smile. This book will show you how!

Because of the huge variety of shapes, sizes, materials, and techniques involved, making lampshades is never boring. Creating a useful 3D object that takes on a different quality when the light shines through it is fulfilling and fascinating—especially when you see how what you have made can set the mood of a room, making your living space feel cozy, quirky, traditional, modern, homespun, or welcoming—depending on its shape, size, position, and what it's made from.

Reuse and upcycle materials whenever possible because things with a history have so much more character, and are often better designed and more solidly made than their modern-day equivalents. Not only do you get the individuality of a handmade object, but it's more eco-friendly, too. As well as restoring secondhand frames and using vintage fabrics, this book shows you how to turn other pre-loved objects—such as books, a sewing notions collection, or a box of photographic slides—into stunning lighting features. And it will give you an excellent excuse for rummaging through thrift stores, yard sales, and secondhand stores, which is one of my favorite hobbies.

This book is full of ideas and inspiration for all types of shade—for every room and all levels of craftiness. I've included projects that use a range of techniques, from basic pattern-making, simple sewing, cross stitch, and embroidery to origami, papier mâché, and other paper crafts, to drilling holes in metal objects. There are some lampshades here simple enough for older children to make—and several ideas for lampshades for kids' rooms, too. Lampshades also make great gifts—who would not be delighted to receive a shade tailor-made just for them?

So pick a project that appeals to you and get making. You can follow my instructions to the letter or just use them as inspiration and develop your own designs. Have fun!

Chapter 1
LAMPSHADE KNOW-HOW

Find everything you need to know here, including information on tools and materials as well as four basic shape lampshade projects that, once you have mastered them, you will use again and again.

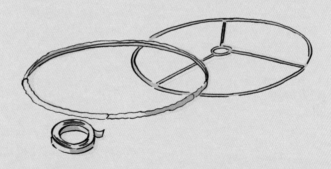

Lampshade shapes

Lampshades come in a whole range of sizes and shapes. The basic frame is what gives a shade its character and to a certain extent will dictate how it can be used—hanging from the ceiling or on a table lamp, as a large feature light in a living room, or as a small bedside lamp.

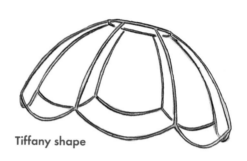

Tiffany shape

Bell shape

Drum shape

Cone shape

A note on size

The size of the piece of fabric and the PVC depends on what size you want your drum lampshade to be. The circumference of the finished shade is obviously determined by the size of the rings you are using—they are available in anything from a dinky 3 in. (8 cm) to a huge 40 in. (1 m) in diameter, so take your pick! But the height is variable, so play around with proportions by roughly wrapping your fabric round one of the rings and securing with clothes pegs until you get a height that looks right with the size of your rings. As a very rough guide, start with a height that is a few inches (centimeters) less than the diameter of the ring. Both drum and cone-shaped shades can look interesting as very tall or short and squat, so experiment and see what works with your living space and what looks good with the base you are planning to use.

Frames can be straight-sided, tapered, hexagonal, scalloped and often have names like "empire," "coolie," or "pagoda" but this book uses just four basic shapes: drum, bell, tiffany, and cone.

The simplest traditional shape is the drum shade, which is essentially a cylinder created by having two rings of the same size at the top and bottom of the shade. A cone shade also uses two rings but the top ring is smaller in diameter. Both the drum and the cone shape can be made using self-adhesive lampshade PVC covered in fabric—there is no sewing involved, just accurate measuring, cutting, and sticking. Tiffany and bell-shaped shades use an entirely different process, involving making fabric templates to fit over an existing frame, hand stitching, and lots of pinning.

Tools and materials

Lampshade rings

To make a drum or cone lampshade you will need a pair of rings, one with a gimbal (see right). These come in different sizes—remember that for a drum shade you need two rings that are the same size but for a cone shade one must be smaller than the other. Lampshade rings can be found from specialist lampshade suppliers (see page 126) and are usually made of strong wire that is painted white to prevent rusting, or plastic-coated. However, you can also use the rings from a pre-used cylindrical or cone shade, although you may need to strip them down and repaint.

Self-adhesive lampshade PVC

Lampshade PVC is a great way to make simple drum and cone shades. A self-adhesive layer is bonded onto PVC, which is then used to form rigid lampshades. Fabric and other materials can be applied to the "peel-back" self-adhesive side, making it heatproof and safe to use. Most products have a grid on one side to help with accurate measuring and cutting. It is available as white or transparent—the project and its design will usually dictate which one you need. If you are making just one shade it can be economical to buy a kit that includes everything you need except the fabric, but if you plan to make more than one shade it is better to buy the PVC on a roll. You can make around five average-sized (10 in./25 cm diameter) drum shades from 40 in. (1 m) of PVC.

What on earth is a gimbal?

Of the two rings in a drum or cone-shaped shade, one needs to have a gimbal—a smaller ring for the light fitting to sit on that is attached to the ring with metal struts or arms. In many cases this is recessed to sit lower than the outside ring. When making your drum or cone lampshade, be sure to position the gimbal pointing inward, not protruding over the edge of the fabric. If you are making a ceiling light, the ring that has the gimbal should be positioned at the top; if you are making a table lamp the gimbal should be positioned at the bottom. This is particularly important if your shade has a design or fabric pattern that needs to be viewed the right way up. However, if you have a hinged gimbal you can flip it round and use it for a ceiling or table lamp as you wish.

Some of the projects in this book involve hanging or fixing objects to a top ring only (see Hanging keys on page 100 and Photographic slides on page 114). For these projects you will need a ring called a "slip uno fitter," also known as a shade carrier. This has very long gimbal arms that extend from the smaller ring around the light fitting up to the top ring. You can buy these online but you may also be able to find them in thrift or secondhand stores.

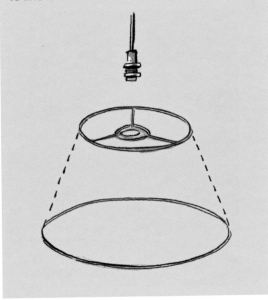

Double-stick lampshade tape

This strong, double-sided tape is used to cover the outside of your lampshade rings, allowing them to be rolled onto the prepared sheet of PVC. It is also used to hold the finished shade together—I usually use two adjacent strips on the overlap for extra holding power. It comes in a variety of widths but I find that ¼ in. (6 mm) is just right.

Basic equipment

Most of the lampshades in this book require a basic craft kit: sharp scissors (for paper and fabric), a cutting mat and craft knife, a tape measure, ruler, needles, threads, pencil, tailor's chalk, and pins. See the individual projects for more details, as some require specific tools such as a drill, can opener, or pliers.

Fabrics

When it comes to fabrics, medium-weight cotton is the most straightforward to work with, although upholstery-weight fabric is also good. Loosely woven fabric with a bit of texture, such as burlap, looks great with the light shining through, although if you have something very loosely woven, you will need to allow for extra large borders to accommodate the inevitable fraying. It's best to avoid stretchy fabric or anything silky that "moves." Tweed or other thick fabrics can make great lampshades, but if you want to make a drum or cone-shaped shade from this type of fabric, you will need to allow an extra ¾ in. (2 cm) overlap, making any overlap 1 ¼ in. (3 cm) in total.

Decorative trims

Decorative trims such as pompom trim, ricrac, braid, and ribbons can really add the right finishing touch to a beautiful handmade lampshade. Look in sewing notions (haberdashery) stores or secondhand vintage stores.

Sourcing vintage materials

Although you can use almost any type of fabric for making lampshades, old vintage fabrics look lovely and will give your lampshades a truly original feel. I think the best prints are those from the mid-twentieth century, although you can find some good copies around these days. You may already have offcuts of fabric from other sewing projects at home but old curtains and unused lengths of fabric can be found at thrift stores, garage or yard sales, and vintage fairs. You could also try specialist vintage shops and online stockists (see page 126). Be creative and make textile lampshades from dish towels, sheets, tablecloths, silk scarves, and hankies—even old clothes. Many of the projects in this book will show you how to turn other beautiful pre-loved objects, including old wooden rulers, children's picture books, old maps, metal sweet molds, cookie tins, and old keys into unique and beautiful lampshades for your home.

Using old lampshade frames

Using an existing lampshade frame has its advantages—you don't need to use specialist materials such as lampshade PVC or double-stick tape and the shapes often have a lovely retro feel. Vintage bell shades and tiffany-paneled shades are often easier to come by than new ones—and usually much nicer. You may have an old shade at home that you are bored with and can re-cover, or perhaps you've seen a dusty secondhand shade, discarded in a yard sale. You need to be able to see the potential of the frame beneath its nasty polyester cover. When you start looking, you'll be amazed at the variety of frame shapes, sizes, and styles!

To strip a shade down to its frame, make a snip in the fabric with some scissors and tear it away from the frame, being careful not to tug too hard or you may pull the frame out of shape. Discard the old fabric, then use a paintstripping tool and/or some sandpaper to deal with any rough bits on the frame (lighter fuel is useful for removing sticky glue). Then, if necessary, repaint the frame—a couple of coats of spray paint is all it takes. Most bought frames are painted white but you can choose to paint yours any color—a pastel or neon color can look stunning.

A drum shade—where the top and bottom rings are the same diameter—is probably the simplest shade to start with and is ideal for both pendant lights and table lamps.

Drum lampshade

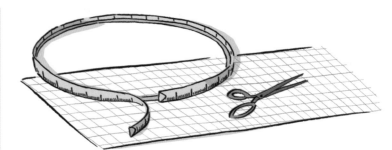

1 Measure round one of your rings with a tape measure to get the circumference and add on ⅝ in. (1.5 cm). Decide how tall you want your shade to be and cut a piece of lampshade PVC to these dimensions.

2 Roughly cut out your chosen fabric, using the piece of lampshade PVC as a guide. You need a border of at least ¾ in. (2 cm) on each long side and ⅜ in. (1 cm) on one short side. But at this point add a few extra inches (centimetres) all round.

3 Lay the PVC on the wrong side of the fabric—if the fabric has a pattern, use it to make sure the PVC is straight. Peel off the first 4 in. (10 cm) of backing paper and with your left hand (or whichever you're comfortable with), stick the PVC down onto the center of your fabric, keeping it as straight as possible. With your right hand, gradually pull out the backing paper as you press and smooth with your left hand.

why not

Decorate a plain shade with pompom trim, ricrac, or ribbon using double-stick tape.

4 Trim the fabric, leaving a ¾ in. (2 cm) border along each long side and a ⅜ in. (1 cm) border along one short side. The other short side should be trimmed right to the edge of the PVC.

5 Stick a piece of double-stick tape along the short edge of the PVC that has the ⅜ in. (1 cm) border, going over the ¾ in. (2 cm) borders at each end. Remove the backing and fold the ⅜ in. (1 cm) border over onto it. Stick another piece of sticky tape right on the folded edge and another one right next to it (but not over). Leave the backing on for now.

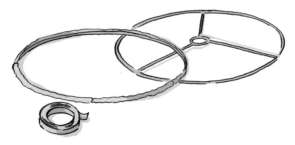

6 Stick double-stick tape around the outsides of both rings but don't remove the backing just yet.

7 If your fabric has a pattern that needs to be the right way up, decide if you are making a table or ceiling lamp and put the ring with the gimbal at the bottom for a table lamp and top for ceiling. In all cases, the gimbal should be facing the inside of the lampshade, so that it doesn't stick out beyond the fabric.

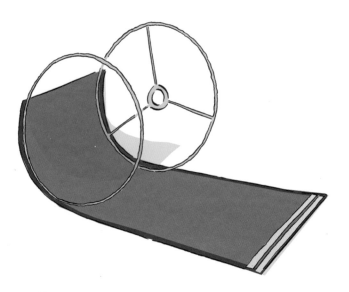

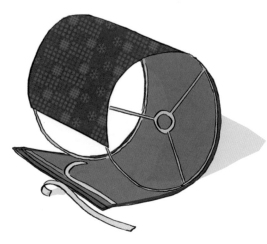

8 Remove the backing from rings. Starting at the opposite end to the one that is folded over, place both rings right on the very edge of the PVC. With one hand on each, carefully roll them at the same time, keeping to the very edges of the PVC. Stop about 1 ¼ in. (3 cm) from the end.

9 Peel off the backing from the tape on the overlap and continue rolling the rings onto the tape. Press down from the inside and you should get a nice neat join.

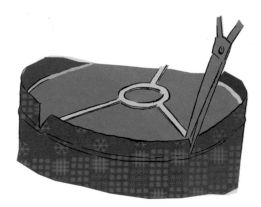

10 Snip the fabric in three places next to the gimbal struts and roughly fold the fabric top and bottom onto the inside.

11 Now you want to tuck the excess fabric under the rings all round top and bottom to create a neat rolled edge. Take an old credit card or store card and use the corner to poke all the excess fabric behind the rings all the way round. You need to be quite forceful so don't worry if you hear clicking sounds.

why not

Use plain fabric for the outside
and a patterned fabric for
the lining.

Master this traditional method and breathe new life into a pre-loved lampshade by covering it with some dazzling new fabric.

Classic lined bell shade

You will need

- Secondhand bell-shaped lampshade frame, stripped and cleaned
- Bias binding or wide cotton tape in a neutral color, ⅜ in. (1 cm) wide
- Fabric—lightweight cotton, satin, or silk (avoid stripes)
- Dressmaker's pins
- Tailor's chalk or soft pencil
- Sewing machine
- Matching sewing thread
- Thimble (optional)
- Cotton or silk lining fabric in white or another color
- Bias binding to match your lining
- Double-stick lampshade tape, ¼ in. (6 mm) wide, or strong white glue
- Decorative trim for the lower edge, such as pompom or fringe, on tape at least ¼ in. (7.5 mm) wide
- Plain trim for top

1 Start by covering the top and bottom rings of the frame, as well as two opposite vertical struts, with bias binding or cotton tape. This is to provide a base to stitch the fabric to. Work out how much bias binding or tape you need by adding twice the circumference of the top and bottom rings and four times the length of one vertical strut. Wind the tape around the top ring where it meets a vertical strut (choose a vertical strut next to the gimbal if yours are positioned this way), overlapping each twist of tape. Cover the top ring, then go down the vertical strut, round the bottom ring and then finish off by covering the facing vertical strut in the same way. Tie off the ends securely and finish off with a couple of tiny stitches to secure.

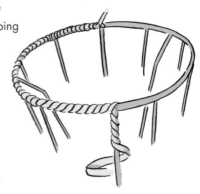

2 To work out how much fabric you need, measure one vertical strut and add 4 in. (10 cm), then measure the circumference of the bottom ring and add on 5 in. (12.5 cm). Cut a rectangle of fabric to this size from both the main fabric and the lining fabric.

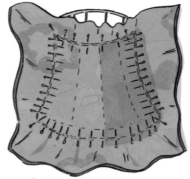

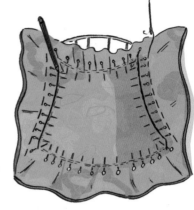

3 Fold your fabric in half, short edges and right sides together, and with the straight of grain running vertically, pin the fabric to half the frame at the four corners where the two bound side struts join the top and bottom rings. Gently stretch this double layer of fabric to the sides, and pin it to the two vertical struts, stretching the fabric taut and adjusting the pins as you go.

4 Pin the fabric to the top and bottom rings in the same way, gently stretching the fabric and adjusting pins to remove any wrinkles until it is perfectly smooth. Keep the sharp ends of pins on the outside so you don't scratch your fingers.

5 Once your fabric is smooth, take your tailor's chalk or soft pencil and mark along the vertical struts between the pins, extending the lines ⅝ in. (1.5 cm) beyond the top and bottom rings. Mark the top and bottom rings in the same way. Without removing the fabric from the frame, tack the two layers of fabric together ¾ in. (2 cm) outside the lines and remove all the pins.

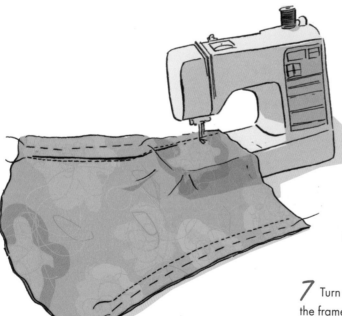

6 Remove the fabric from the frame and, using a sewing machine, stitch down the vertical tailor's chalk lines. Trim the vertical seam allowances to ¼ in. (5 mm) but leave at least 1¼ in. (3 cm) excess outside the top and bottom (horizontal) chalk lines. Press the seams open. Make the lining in exactly the same way.

7 Turn the outer fabric right side out and slip it over the frame, lining up the side seams with the two bound struts and the horizontal lines with the top and bottom rings. Adjust to fit snugly and pin in place.

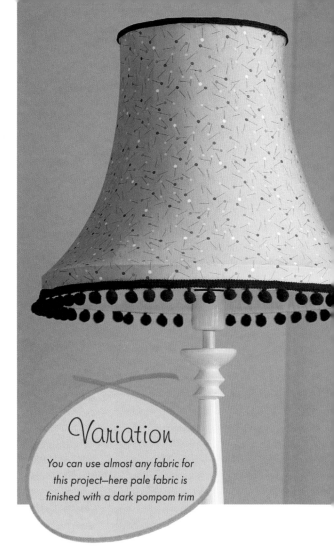

8 Using double thread, stitch the cover to the frame along the top and bottom rings, keeping the stitches to the outside. Trim away excess fabric close to stitching.

9 If your frame has a gimbal that joins in two places, simply unpick the top of the side seams by ¾ in. (2 cm) to accommodate the gimbal. If your frame has a gimbal that joins the frame in more than two places, turn the shade upside down and drop the lining in, matching the side seams with the bound struts. With a pencil or tailor's chalk, mark on your lining where the gimbal struts fall, cut ¾ in. (2 cm) slits, and finish them off with matching bias binding. Carefully trim away the excess fabric as close to the stitching as you can.

Variation

You can use almost any fabric for this project—here pale fabric is finished with a dark pompom trim

10 Press the lining and place it inside the frame. Pin securely and stitch it in place in the same way as you did the outer fabric, keeping the stitching to the outside so it is covering the stitching on the outer fabric as much as possible.

11 Cut your chosen trim to the circumference of each ring, adding ⅜ in. (1 cm) for overlap. Using double-stick tape or strong glue, attach to the bottom of the frame to cover all stitching. Repeat with a matching plain trim at the top ring.

This shape takes its name from the famous glass lamps designed by Louis Comfort Tiffany's design studio, now associated with the Art Nouveau movement. This classic method involves covering the shade, with its scalloped edge, with fabric panels

Tiffany paneled shade

1 Take an old tiffany-shaped frame and strip it down, removing any glue and chipped paint. Sand and repaint if necessary. On a flat surface, lay the frame on a piece of scrap fabric and, with tailor's chalk, draw around the outside of one section—you will need to roll the frame slightly to draw the top and bottom edges. Take care to keep it lined up as you do this.

2 Take the frame away and, with tailor's chalk, add ½ in. (1 cm) to the sides and top of the panel shape and ¾ in. (2 cm) to the scalloped bottom edge. Cut out along these lines. Using this shape as a template, cut eight (or however many sections your frame has) pieces from your chosen fabric.

why not

Make each panel from a different fabric for a patchwork effect.

3 Using your sewing machine, stay stitch along the top edges of each panel to prevent stretching: simply machine stitch a line ¼ in. (5 mm) from the raw edge. Start stitching the panels together using French seams: place the first and second panels together, wrong sides together, and stitch ¼ in (5 mm) away from the edge down one side. Trim the seam allowance to ⅛ in. (3 mm), press the seam open and then turn right sides together. Press along the seam and stitch again, ¼ in (5 mm) away from the edge. Continue until you have joined all the panels together and press all the seams to the same side.

4 Trim the top edge by ¼ in. (5 mm). Open out the bias binding and pin the narrow edge to the top of the fabric panels, right sides together. Stitch along the crease and then fold the tape over to the reverse and slip stitch in place. Attach the first panel to the eighth with another French seam.

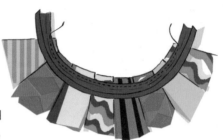

5 Place the cover over your frame, aligning the seams with the struts and tucking them under—it should fit nice and snugly. Pull down each panel, turn under the ¾ in. (2 cm) excess at the bottom edge to the inside and pin through both layers of fabric securely all around.

6 With a double length of matching sewing thread, hand stitch the hem, just inside the bottom of the frame, using running or slip stitch.

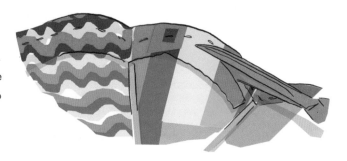

7 Trim the excess fabric as close to the stitching as you can, being careful not to cut the stitching.

8 Stick double-stick tape (or use clear-drying glue) onto the reverse of a long strip of bias binding. Stick to the inside of the lampshade to hide all the stitching, stretching as you go to fit around each scalloped edge. Attach fringeing or pompom edging to the outside in the same way, neatening the end by folding over and sticking with a tiny piece of tape.

A cone lampshade simply has a top ring that is smaller than the bottom ring and can be made as shallow or tall as you choose. This fairly classic table lamp is finished with a ribbon trim in a bright contrasting color.

Classic cone with neon trim

1 Measure the diameter of the bottom ring and draw a line to this length in the bottom right corner of your pattern paper (line A). Decide how tall you want your lampshade to be and draw a vertical line through the center of line A (line B). Measure the diameter of the top ring and draw another horizontal line to this length, centered at the top of line B (line C).

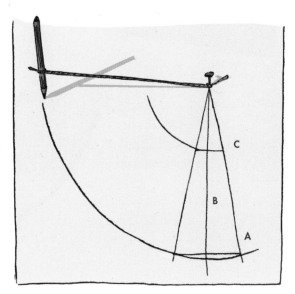

Use a ruler to join the ends of line A to the ends of line C and continue these lines upward until they meet at the top. Pin the end of a length of string where these long lines meet and stretch it down to the right-hand end of line A. Tie the string round the pencil so the point of the pencil touches this point and, keeping the string taut and pencil upright, carefully draw an arc that is the length of the circumference of the bottom ring (check it with a tape measure). Draw a second, smaller arc starting from the right-hand end of line C, the length of the circumference of the top ring. Add ¾ in. (2 cm) to both arcs for the overlap and join them up.

2 Cut out this template and use it to cut out the shape from lampshade PVC.

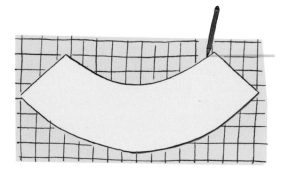

3 Lay the PVC on the wrong side of the fabric. Peel off the first 4 in. (10 cm) of backing paper and with your left hand (or whichever you're comfortable with), stick the PVC down onto the center of your fabric, keeping it as straight as possible. With your right hand, gradually pull out the backing paper as you press and smooth with your left hand.

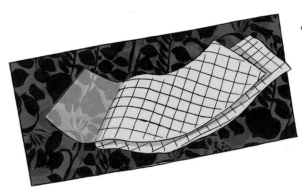

4 Trim the fabric, leaving a border of ¾ in. (2 cm) along both curved edges and ⅜ in. (1 cm) along one short end. The other short end should be trimmed right to the edge of the PVC. Stick a piece of double-stick tape down the edge of the PVC next to the ⅜ in. (1 cm) border and fold the border down onto it. Stick another piece of tape along the very edge of the fold.

5 Cover the outside of both rings with double-stick tape and peel off the top layer. Starting at the end with no border, roll the smaller one along the shorter curve, at the same time rolling the larger one along the long curve. Stick to the very edges of the PVC (don't stray onto the fabric) and stop about 1¼ in. (3 cm) from the end. Peel off the top layer of tape from the short edge and continue rolling the rings onto it. Press down from the inside.

6 Snip the fabric at the top to accommodate the gimbal struts and then roughly fold the fabric top and bottom to the inside.

7 Tuck the excess fabric under the rings all round top and bottom to create a neat rolled edge. Take an old credit card or store card and use the corner to poke all the excess fabric behind the rings all the way round. Stick the ribbon trim to the top and bottom edges of the shade, using double-stick tape or PVA adhesive.

why not
Play with the height of the shade, making it very tall or shallow.

Chapter 2
TEXTILES

Textiles are an obvious choice for lampshades but this chapter uses all manner of fabrics, including embroidery, cross stitch, ribbon, lace, doilies—even your favorite sweater—to make beautiful lampshades.

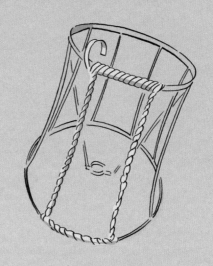

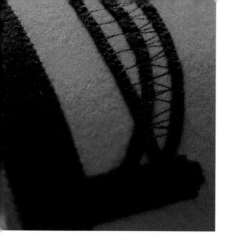

Turn a simple drum shade into something special! This striking lampshade has famous landmarks from around the world set against a stunning red background.

Appliqué skyline

1 On the right side of your main fabric, mark out a rectangle in tailor's chalk that is 38 × 10 in. (97 × 25 cm)—this is the circumference of your rings plus ¾ in. (2 cm) for the overlap by the height you want the lampshade to be (10 in./25 cm in this case). Cut out this rectangle, leaving at least 2 in. (5 cm) all around.

2 Trace the outlines of the building templates onto the paper backing of your Bondaweb pieces, adding a base that is ¾ in. (2 cm) high and that extends for 2 in. (5 cm) from each side of the building (these will join up to create a solid border around the bottom edge of the lampshade).

3 Fuse the Bondaweb onto pieces of black felt by gently pressing with a hot iron for about 10 seconds. Carefully cut out each building shape, including the base.

You will need

20 in. (50 cm) medium-weight fabric, such as non-stretch wool

Tailor's chalk

Tape measure

Scissors

Templates on page 123

20 in. (50 cm) Bondaweb

20 in. (50 cm) black felt

Sewing machine

Needle and black sewing thread

20 in. (50 cm) clear self-adhesive lampshade PVC

Pair of drum lampshade rings, 12 in. (30 cm) in diameter

Double-stick lampshade tape, ¼ in. (6 mm) wide

An old store card or library card

4 Arrange the felt building shapes along the lower edge of the marked out rectangle. Trim the sides of bases so they are evenly spaced and fit exactly along the rectangle. Peel off the Bondaweb paper and with a hot iron, press each building onto the right side of your fabric, making sure you keep each base flush with the next and lined up along the tailor's chalk line.

5 Using black sewing thread and a short zigzag stitch, machine stitch around the outlines of all the buildings, leaving as much detail as possible. Zigzag right along the edges of the border and down the joins between the bases. Then stitch any details, such as aerials, or the spokes of the London Eye, using straight stitch or by hand. Neaten all loose ends.

6 Cut a piece of PVC to the same size as your original rectangle, including the overlap, and stick to your fabric, taking care to align one long edge just below the bases of the buildings. Follow the instructions for the Drum Lampshade on pages 14–17 to make up your lampshade. The buildings should be neatly lined up along the lower edge of your lampshade.

why not

Make up templates of buildings in your local area by tracing the outlines from photographs.

why not

Instead of using all different fabrics, alternate between just two or three colors. Adapt the color and style to suit your own room.

These gorgeous fairy lights are easy to make and look so pretty draped over a bed frame, around a mirror, or simply hung on your wall. Made from plastic party cups, scraps of vintage fabric, and oddments of decorative trim, they will create a totally unique lighting look.

Vintage fabric fairy lights

1 Trim your plastic cups to the size required. I used 10 oz (330 ml) cups which were quite tall so I cut off the tops down to one of the ridges. You will also need to cut a cross about ⅜ in. (1 cm) wide in the base of each cup. Push a thick darning needle or wooden skewer through the center of the base to make a hole and then use small sharp scissors to make four ¼ in. (5 mm) snips in a cross shape.

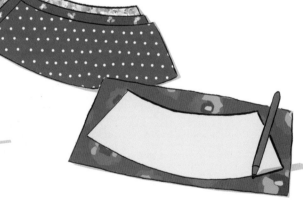

2 To make a template, roll one cup along a piece of A4 paper and follow the top and bottom edge with a pencil. Make a mark on the base of the cup first so you know when you have rolled once round. Add ⅜ in. (1 cm) to one end, cut out your shape and wrap it round the cup to see if it fits. If not, repeat the process until you get it right. When you're happy with the fit, draw around your paper template on card and cut out.

3 Use the cardboard template to cut out the shape from several different fabric scraps; draw around the template first using a fabric marker pen. Continue until you have enough to make a shade for each bulb on your string of fairy lights.

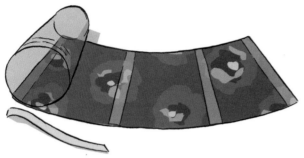

4 Stick four strips of double-stick tape onto the wrong side of your first fabric piece—one at each short end and two toward the center. Peel the backing off the tape and wrap the piece of fabric around a cup, pressing down to stick. Repeat with the remaining pieces of fabric and cups until you have your desired number of fairy light shades.

5 Turn under the ⅜ in. (1 cm) overlap and stick down with more double-stick tape. Measure the diameter of the open end of the cup and add ⅜ in. (1 cm). Cut a piece of your chosen trimming to this length and, starting at the point where the fabric overlaps, attach to the very edge of the shade using double-stick tape.

6 Pop a fairy-light bulb through the cross in the base of each cup.

This is such a simple idea but is so effective, playing on the idea of lights within a light. By cutting away small areas of the PVC lining, you can create the effect of lighted windows, which is only revealed when the lamp is turned on. This would work well with a darker colored fabric, too.

Decoupage windows

You will need

Pair of drum lampshade rings

Tape measure

Sheet of self-adhesive white lampshade PVC

Pencil, ruler, eraser

Scalpel and cutting board

Solid-colored cotton fabric

Scissors

Double-stick lampshade tape, ¼ in. (6 mm) wide

An old store card or library card

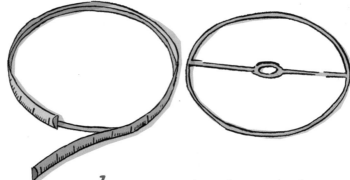

1 Measure around one of your rings with a tape measure to get the circumference and add on ⅝ in. (1.5 cm). Decide how tall you want your shade to be and cut a piece of lampshade PVC to these dimensions.

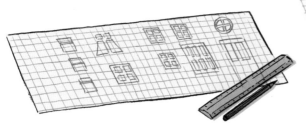

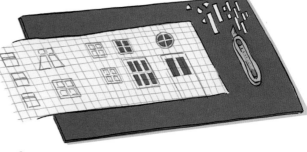

2 With a pencil and ruler, and using the grid on the backing of the PVC to help you, draw different-shaped windows and doors on the paper side of the PVC. Make sure you leave a border of at least ¾ in. (2 cm) uncut at the top and bottom.

3 When you are happy with your layout of window shapes, take a scalpel, ruler, and cutting mat and carefully cut out the shapes. If you have drawn a block of windows, as if in an apartment, leave a couple of windows uncut, so it looks as if the lights are off. Use the eraser to rub out any pencil marks.

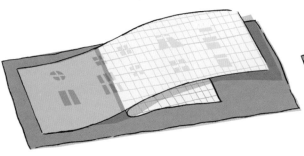
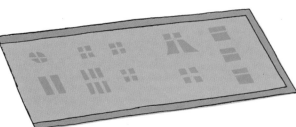

4 Roughly cut your chosen fabric to the dimensions of your PVC rectangle, adding a few inches (centimetres) all around; press. Lay the PVC on the wrong side of the fabric. Peel off the first 4 in. (10 cm) of the backing paper and with your left hand, stick the PVC down onto the fabric, keeping it as straight as possible. With your right hand, gradually pull the backing paper as you press and smooth with your left hand.

5 Trim the fabric, leaving a ¾ in. (2 cm) border along each long side and a ⅜ in. (1 cm) border along one short side. The other short side should be trimmed right to the edge of the PVC.

6 Make up the lampshade following steps 5–11 of the Drum Lampshade on pages 14–17.

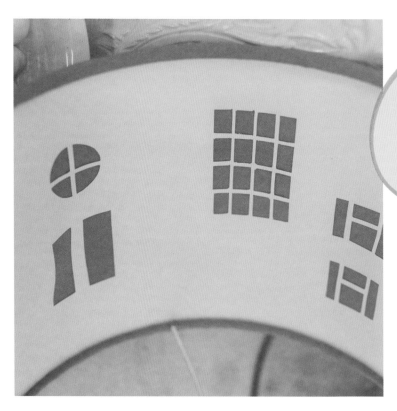

why not

Be inspired by your own house or the windows of buildings on your street.

A very easy way to cover a bell-shaped frame. Look for ribbon with a pretty pattern—although striped or plain ribbon would also work well.

Twisted ribbon

1 If your ribbon is not on a roll, wrap it into a loose bunch and secure with an elastic band so you can work with it more easily, letting out lengths as you need them.

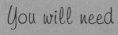
2 Tuck the end of the ribbon around the top ring of the frame, pin in place, and secure with a couple of neat stitches. Twist the ribbon twice counterclockwise and pass the bundle or roll of ribbon round the bottom of the frame and up the inside of the frame. Slightly overlap the first piece at the top, twist twice and pass down the inside of the shade again. Pull the ribbon fairly taut as you go.

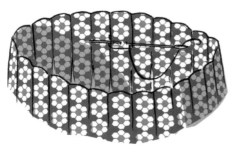

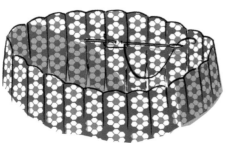

3 Continue in this way, overlapping a little at the top and spacing evenly at the bottom until you get back to where you started. Trim the final length of ribbon to about 1 in. (2.5 cm), turn the end under and stitch neatly to one of the ribbon twists on the inside to secure.

why not

Use wider ribbon—the wider it is,
the less you will need. Alternatively
you can experiment with the
number of twists.

This is a great project if you have an old bell-shaped lampshade that needs updating. Ideally you want to find one that has a separate wired section around the bottom—you should be able to feel it through the fabric. It is also perfect for using up oddments of yarn.

Wrapped yarn shade

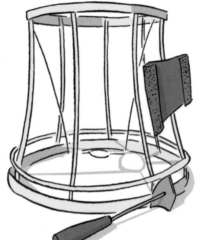

1 If you are using an old lampshade, remove the old fabric from the frame by cutting with scissors and pulling it away. Remove any chipped or peeling paint with a paint scraper and sand down the frame if necessary to remove any rough bits.

2 Choose a yarn color to cover the top ring of the frame and tie one end onto to the frame to secure. Start winding it around so that no part of the frame is showing. When you get to the end, cut the yarn and tie the end to the frame.

3 If you have a frame with separate sections around the bottom, wrap these next. Make a small ball of yarn, which is easier to handle than a full ball, and turn the frame upside down so that you don't have to keep lifting up the shade. Tie the end to one of the struts and start wrapping vertically to fill the space, passing the ball of yarn through the frame as you go. You don't need to keep within the sections—just keep going until you have covered a strip of the desired length. Tie off the end. Continue around the bottom sections of the frame in the same way, making strips of random lengths from different colors of yarn.

4 Fill the large panels in the same way, wrapping yarn horizontally this time and adding texture by overlapping some "threads" rather than making it perfectly neat. Fill alternate panels, some with one complete color or with two colors for a block effect. Tie the ends as you go and leave the lengths of ends to sew in later.

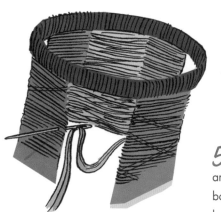

5 To fill in the panels that are still open you will need a bodkin. Take a very long length of your chosen yarn and thread the bodkin. Start at the inside top of the lampshade and use the bodkin to thread the yarn through two strands of yarn, just next to one of the struts. As if you are making a long "stitch," bring the yarn back between two strands of yarn outside the opposite strut. Work your way down the panel in the same way, crossing over in some places like you did before to add texture.

why not

Wind the yarn more loosely, leaving gaps so that more light shines through. If you do this, you may need to paint your frame with white gloss or spray paint and leave to dry thoroughly before you start.

6 When all the panels are filled and no part of the frame is visible, check that all the loose ends are tied securely. Use the bodkin to thread them through where they can't be seen, before snipping off.

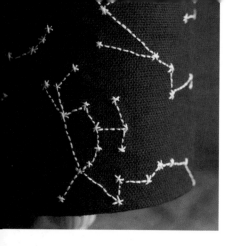

A simple drum shade in a dark fabric is decorated with constellations from the night sky—perfect for a budding astronomer's bedroom.

Starry night

You will need

Pair of drum lampshade rings
(I used 10 in./25 cm here)

Tape measure

White self-adhesive lamp-
shade PVC

Scissors

Dark blue fabric, such as a
linen silk mix

Sewing thread in a
contrasting color

Night sky diagram

Tailor's chalk

Embroidery hoop

Three skeins of white
stranded embroidery floss
(cotton)

Embroidery needle

Double-stick lampshade tape,
¼ in. (6 mm) wide

An old store card or
library card

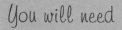

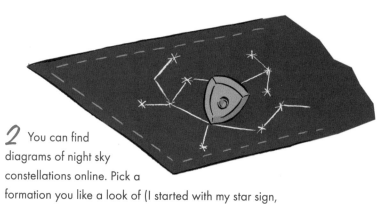

1 Referring to the instructions for the Drum Lampshade on pages 14–17, work out the dimensions of the sheet of PVC you will need, according to the size of your rings. Mark out this area on your dark fabric, using a large running stitch and sewing thread in a bright color.

2 You can find diagrams of night sky constellations online. Pick a formation you like a look of (I started with my star sign, Gemini) and, using tailor's chalk, draw the lines onto your fabric, keeping within the running stitch border.

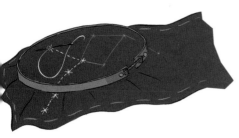

3 Place the marked section of fabric into an embroidery hoop and backstitch along the lines using white embroidery floss (cotton), stopping at each corner to make a star from three straight stitches crossing at the center. Remove the fabric from the hoop and draw your next constellation in tailor's chalk, keeping within the border, repeating until your piece of fabric is evenly covered. Feel free to use some artistic licence to create a pleasing arrangement! Secure the ends of the embroidery floss (cotton) by weaving the ends back through the stitching and trim to neaten.

4 Make up the lampshade following steps 3–11 of the Drum Lampshade on pages 14–17.

why not

Add a couple of stars in silver or gold thread.

This inexpensive, rough-textured fabric looks great with the light shining through it—here it's contrasted with bright-colored felt shapes and fine gold stitching.

Embellished burlap

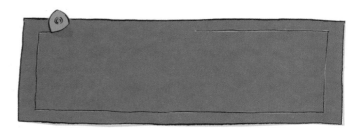

1 Referring to the instructions for the Drum Lampshade on pages 14–17, measure your rings, calculate the size of PVC you will need, and mark the shape on the burlap (hessian) using tailor's chalk or a large running stitch. Roughly cut it out, leaving a few inches (centimeters) all round to allow for adjustments and fraying.

You will need

Pair of drum lampshade rings

Tape measure

20 × 40 in. (50 × 100 cm) burlap (hessian) fabric

Ruler

Tailor's chalk

Scissors

Squares of felt in five bright colors

Pins

Gold sewing thread

20 in. (50 cm) transparent self-adhesive lampshade PVC

Double-stick lampshade tape, ¼ in. (6 mm) wide

An old store card or library card

2 Cut out felt triangles 2 in. (5 cm) tall from each color—here I used vertical rows of seven triangles, but you may need more or fewer, depending on the height of your shade.

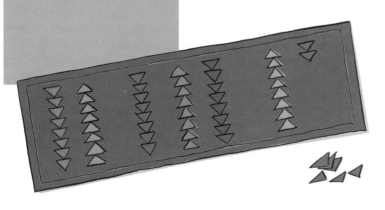

3 Arrange the triangles in vertical rows within the rectangle marked on the burlap. Alternate the colors and place the rows at irregular intervals with one row pointing up and the next row pointing down and so on. Pin each triangle in place.

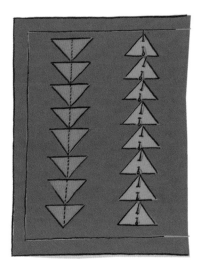

4 Thread your sewing machine with gold thread and stitch in a straight line through the center of your first vertical row of triangles, removing the pins as your go. Repeat for the remaining rows.

5 Make up your shade, referring to steps 3–11 of the Drum Lampshade. Make sure you leave a larger border than usual as this fabric frays very easily!

why not
As this fabric costs next to nothing, try cutting it on the bias so the weave makes diagonal lines.

Give some lovingly made linen a new lease of life by cutting into panels and using it to cover a bell-shaped lampshade frame.

Upcycled vintage tablecloths

1 Launder and press your vintage tablecloth fabric. Prepare your lampshade frame by removing any loose paint and sanding and repainting if necessary. The vertical struts will be visible inside, but the top and bottom rings will be covered in fabric.

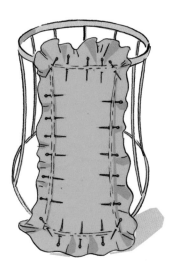

2 Bind one section of your frame, i.e. the two adjacent vertical struts and the top and bottom rings that join them, with bias binding, winding round and overlapping on each turn.

3 Pin your scrap of fabric onto the bound section of the frame, starting at the corners. Pull it taut and pin down the two bound struts and the bound sections of the top and bottom rings.

4 When it is stretched taut, mark the shape of the panel between the pins along the struts and rings with a soft pencil or tailor's chalk.

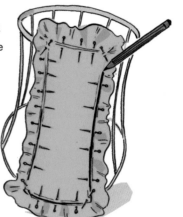

why not
Add vintage lace trim to the lower edge using double-sided tape or glue.

5 Remove the pins and fabric from the frame and cut out the shape, adding ½ in. (1 cm) down each side and ¾ in. (2 cm) at the top and bottom for seam allowances. Remove the binding from frame.

6 Use this fabric template to cut eight panels from your tablecloths, choosing areas with the most interesting embroidered details.

7 Using your sewing machine, stay stitch along the top and bottom edges of each panel to prevent stretching: simply machine stitch a line ⅜ in. (1 cm) from the raw edges. This is particularly necessary if some of your panels are cut on the bias. Start stitching the panels together using French seams: place the first and second panels together, wrong sides together, and stitch ¼ in (5 mm) from the edge down one side. Trim the seam allowance to ⅛ in. (3 mm), press the seam open and then turn right sides together. Press along the seam and stitch again, ¼ in (5 mm) away from the edge.

8 Continue until you have joined all the panels together and press all the seams to the same side. Turn the top and bottom edges under by ⅜ in. (1 cm), press, and stitch. Then join the first panel to the eighth with another French seam. Press the cover, pressing all the seams in the same direction, and pull it down over your over your frame, matching the seams with the vertical struts. Turn the hemmed top and bottom edges over to the inside and pin in place.

9 Using white thread, stitch around the top and bottom edges of the frame using a small running stitch. Stitch as neatly as you can, keeping close to the rings.

Bring an old lampshade from the 1970s right up to date by adding some simple cross stitch in light and bright colors.

Retro wicker shade with cross stitch

1 Decide on the order of your different colors of yarn. You will be using one for each panel so make sure each one looks good with its neighbor.

2 On your first panel, mark a diagonal line of holes in the wicker weave with masking tape, going upper left to lower right.

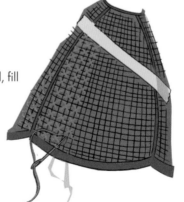

3 Thread the bodkin with your first color of yarn and, starting bottom left of the first panel, fill in a vertical row of the wicker weave in cross stitch. Once you run out of holes, move up one or a few and start cross-stitching the next rown downward. At the bottom, move another row to the right and cross stitch upward—keep doing this until you meet the masking tape line and then move down one cross stitch and stitch downward. Repeat until you have filled in the whole area, tying the yarn at the back when it runs out and sewing in any loose ends.

4 Repeat with the next color on the next panel and continue until all the panels are filled in. Finally, use double-stick tape or clear-drying glue to attach your fringe trim to the lower edge of the shade.

why not

Try filling in whole panels in
one or two colors.

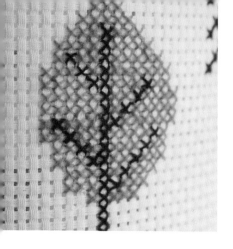

Here's a new use for the fabric you used to do cross stitch on at school—because it's so stiff, you don't need a lining. This campsite scene would look really sweet in a little boy's bedroom.

Cross stitch campsite

Templates on page 124

Here's a new use

You will need

Pair of drum lampshade rings, 10 in. (25 cm) in diameter

Tape measure

20 in. (50 cm) aida fabric

Scissors

Templates on page 124

Yarn or embroidery floss (thread) in various colors

Embroidery needle

Double-stick lampshade tape, ¼ in. (6 mm) wide

An old store or library card

LED or low-wattage bulb

1 To work out the dimensions of the piece of aida that you need, measure the circumference of your rings and add on ⅜ in. (1 cm)— this is the length. Decide how tall you want your shade to be—the one pictured is 6¾ in. (17 cm) tall. Mark out this area on the aida fabric in a loose running stitch and roughly cut out, leaving a few inches (centimeters) all around.

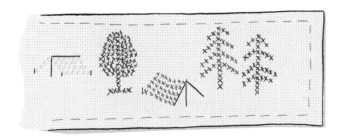

2 Using the templates as a guide and keeping within the running stitch border, cross stitch the two types of tree, the two types of tent, and a campfire. Vary the colors used and position the different elements in a pleasing arrangement. To work a row of cross stitches, work the diagonal stitches in one direction only, then reverse the direction and work the second half of each stitch back across the line. Add any straight line details in straight stitch. Sew in and tie off the ends to keep the back as neat as possible.

3 Remove the running-stitch markers and cut the fabric to the correct size, not forgetting the ⅜ in. (1 cm) you added at one short end for the overlap. Stick a piece of double-stick tape along this short edge.

4 Make up your lampshade following steps 6–9 of the Drum Lampshade on pages 14–17. You won't need PVC backing as the aida is stiff enough, so roll the rings directly onto the edges of the aida. You don't need to fold over the short edge either, as the aida shouldn't fray.

why not

Use black or dark blue aida for a twinkly effect when the light shines through the holes.

why not

Instead of a birdhouse, make a dolls' house by adding felt windows, doors, and other details.

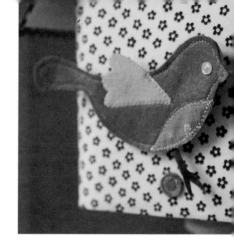

Bring the outdoors in with this cute nesting place, complete with moveable, stick-on feathered friend! Make sure you use an LED or energy-saving light bulb for this shade.

Birdhouse

You will need

Tape measure

Pair of square lampshade rings

Self-adhesive white lampshade PVC

Pencil and ruler

Scissors

Patterned fabric

Scraps of felt in various colors, including black

Scraps of Bondaweb

White sewing thread

Double-stick lampshade tape, ¼ in. (6 mm) wide

An old store or library card

Red fabric

Red decorative trim

Template on page 125

Small button

Velcro dots

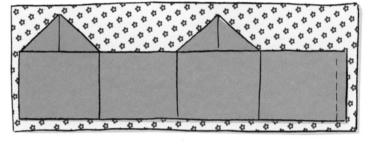

1 Measure one side of your square ring, multiply by four and mark this length on the lower edge of your PVC. Divide the line into four equal parts and then use a ruler to draw straight lines upward from each marked point, the same length as one side of the ring. Draw another long line along the top to create four adjoining squares. Add ⅜ in. (1 cm) at the right-hand short edge for the overlap. Mark the center of the top edge of the first (left-hand) square. From this point, measure up half the original measurement and join up with the corners of the square to form a roof shape. Repeat on the third square.

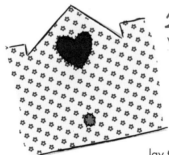

2 Cut out your PVC shape and lay it white (not paper) side down on the right side of your fabric. Roughly cut out the fabric, leaving a generous 2 in. (5 cm) border all round. Cut out a heart shape for the "hole" from black felt and a circle from green felt for a perch, and lay them on the right side of the fabric, positioning the heart toward the top and the circle toward the bottom of where the third square will go. Pin or Bondaweb them in place and zigzag stitch around the edges in white thread. Cut off any loose threads.

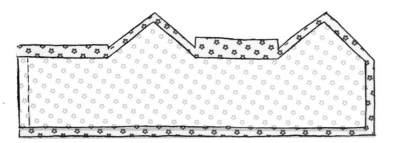

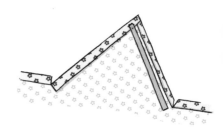

3 Peel the backing off your PVC and stick to the wrong side of your fabric, being careful to keep the hole and perch in the center of the third side of the house. Trim the fabric leaving a ¾ in. (2 cm) border along the bottom edge, a ¼ in. (6 mm) border along the side of the first square, a ¼ in. (6 mm) border along the triangle roof shapes, and a ¾ in. (2 cm) border along the top of the second and fourth squares. The other short edge, with the ⅜ in. (1 cm) overlap, has no border.

4 Snip the borders where the roofs meet the squares and stick double-stick tape on the PVC, along the edges of roofs. Fold the ¼ in. (6 mm) borders onto it to neaten.

5 Stick a piece of tape along the short edge with the fabric border and fold the border over onto it. Stick another piece of tape along the edge but don't remove the backing tape yet. Fold the overlap on the first square inward, so it is roughly at a right angle.

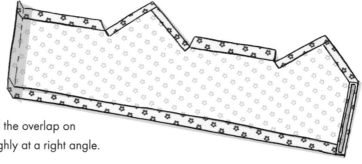

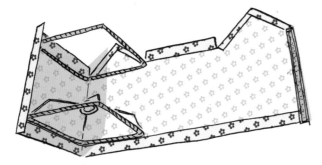

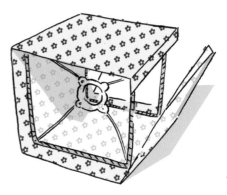

6 Tape the outside of your square rings and peel off the top layer. Starting at the end with the overlap (square 1), stick the lower lampshade ring, with the gimbal toward the inside, on the bottom edge of the PVC with the right angle overlap going round a corner. Stick the top ring at the top, with a corner where the roof starts. Press down to stick and then roll onto the next side of the square, keeping it straight and pressing down firmly.

7 Repeat with the third side. Peel away the backing tape on the fourth square and then stick the fourth square onto the rings, pressing the taped edge firmly onto the overlap to secure.

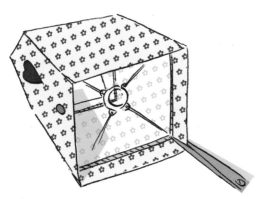

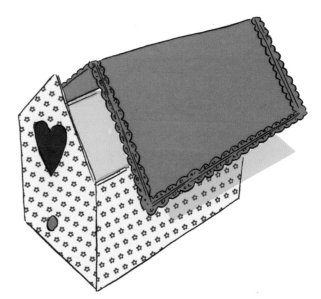

8 Using an old store card, tuck the excess fabric along the upper edges (without roofs) under and behind the rings (see step 11 of the Drum lampshade, page 17). Repeat with the excess fabric along the lower edge—you will need to snip the fabric at the lower corners, or wherever the gimbals join.

9 Now make the roof. To work out the size, measure the side of one roof, double the measurement and add on 1½ in. (4 cm). Measure one side of the house and add on 1¼ in. (3 cm). Cut a piece of lampshade PVC to this size. Peel the backing off the PVC and stick to the wrong side of some red fabric; trim the edges flush with the PVC. Use double-stick tape to add your decorative trim. Make a fold down the middle and set it on top of your birdhouse.

10 To make the bird, use the templates on page 125 to cut two bird shapes, a wing, and a breast shape from felt. Cut a scrap of orange felt for the beak. Machine stitch the two bird shapes together around the edge and then use scraps of Bondaweb to stick the wing and breast shapes to the bird. Zigzag stitch around the shapes to secure. Sew on a small button for the eye and cut some legs from brown felt.

11 Stick one half of a Velcro dot on the back of the bird and the other half on the front of the house. Position another Velcro dot half on the roof so you can move the bird.

This is really simple to make and would look especially lovely in a bedroom. Choose a bright neon color for the ribbon trim to make a real impact.

Lovely lace

You will need

Pair of drum lampshade rings, 8 in. (20 cm) in diameter

40 × 9 in (100 × 22 cm) lace fabric

80 in. (2 m) bright ribbon, ⅜ in. (1 cm) wide

Sewing machine

Needle and white sewing thread

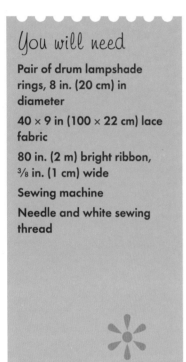

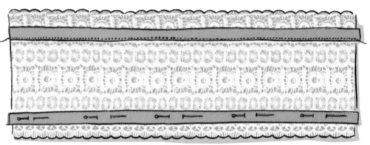

1 Measure the circumference of your lampshade rings and cut your lace panel to this length plus 1½ in. (4 cm). Cut your ribbon into two pieces of the same length. Pin one piece of ribbon ⅜–¾ in. (1–2 cm) in from one long edge of the lace panel, aligning the inner edge of the ribbon with a filled-in (non-holey) part of the lace to give your sewing machine something to grip on to. With white thread, stitch along the inner edge of the ribbon. Attach the other piece of ribbon to the other long edge in the same way.

2 To make a French seam, fold the lace panel in half, short edge to short edge and with wrong sides together (so that the ribbon is on the inside). Pin, making sure that the ribbons are aligned, and then machine stitch, ⅜ in. (1 cm) from the raw edge. Trim the seam to ¼ in. (5 mm) and press the seam open, avoiding the ribbons if they are acrylic and likely to melt—test a scrap first. Turn inside out, so the right sides are now together. Press and stitch again, ⅜ in. (1 cm) in from first seam. Press the seam to one side.

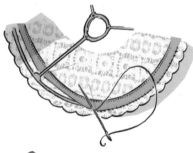

3 Position the top ring—with the gimbal—under the ribbon and, using white sewing thread, slip stitch the upper edge of the ribbon to the lace, forming a channel with the lampshade ring inside.

4 When you get to the gimbal struts, make a small snip in the ribbon, so that it can go either side of the strut. You will also need to unpick a small section of the French seam to accommodate the metal ring. Repeat on the bottom ring—this is much easier as there is no gimbal to get in the way!

why not

Stitch together tiers of narrower lace for a really interesting texture.

why not

Re-cover an existing plain drum lampshade in the same way. Simply prepare your fabric as described, making a "tube" to slip over the shade and gathering the top and bottom edges.

If you've accidently shrunk your favorite sweater in the wash—don't throw it away, here's a new use for it. Here I have made use of the decorative border on an old fair isle sweater.

Felted fair isle

You will need

A woolen sweater (at least 90% wool)
Pair of drum lampshade rings
Self-adhesive lampshade PVC
Sharp scissors
Sewing machine
Matching sewing thread
Tailor's chalk or pins
Double-stick lampshade tape, ¼ in. (6 mm) wide

1 Even if your sweater is already shrunk, felt it by washing it in the washing machine on a hot (90°C) wash. Leave to dry. This will prevent it from fraying when cut.

2 Referring to the instructions for the Drum Lampshade on pages 14–17, measure your rings, calculate the size of PVC you will need, and cut out. You will also need to cut out a strip from your sweater to this measurement plus ⅜ in. (1 cm) along both long edges. To do this, cut off the lower part of the sweater (through both layers) and then cut off one of the side seams. Open out the strip.

3 If the strip lies straight, you will simply need to trim the top and side edges to fit, but if the sweater was shaped and tapered toward the bottom edge, you will need to make the strip straight by adjusting the existing seam. Fold the strip in half, right sides together and then, using a sewing machine, sew a new straight side seam next to the old one. Trim away the excess fabric from the seam.

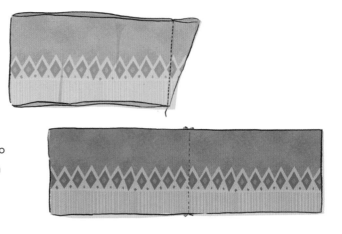

4 Press your strip of fabric on the reverse and then, with tailor's chalk or pins, mark out an area which is ⅜ in. (1 cm) wider than the PVC along both long edges and flush with the PVC along both short edges. Use your sewing machine to zigzag stitch along these lines and then trim the sweater fabric close to the stitching.

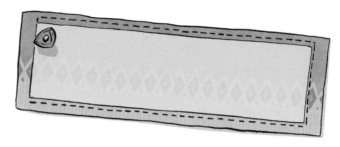

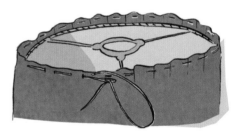

5 Peel the backing off your PVC and stick it to the wrong side of your sweater strip, taking care to keep it straight. Stick double-stick tape around the outside of both lampshade rings, and a strip down one short end of the PVC, then roll the rings along the long edges of the PVC. Just before you get to the end, peel the backing off the tape and roll onto it. Press down to stick.

6 Using a double length of matching sewing thread, stitch a long running stitch around the ⅜ in. (1 cm) of excess fabric, close to the top edge where you zigzag stitched. Pull the threads tight to gather the fabric and then sew in the ends. Repeat around the bottom edge.

7 Finally, slip stitch down the side seam to secure.

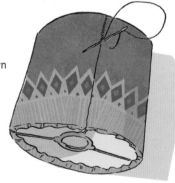

Turning flat, lace doilies into a solid 3D creation is so satisfying and, once hung up, this pretty pendant shade makes the loveliest shadows on the wall. Choose doilies that are not too delicate and open.

Delicate doilies

You will need

Newspaper
Inflatable beach ball
Small cardboard box to stand the ball in
Wallpaper paste
10–15 round lace doilies
Paintbrush
Strong white glue
Small lampshade ring, about 5 in. (12 cm) in diameter

1 Cover your working area with newspaper—this gets messy! Inflate your beach ball and position the ball in the box, valve pointing downward. Make up a bowl of wallpaper paste to a fairly thick consistency.

2 Cut the center out of a round doily to make a hole about 4 in. (10 cm) in diameter (or slightly smaller than your lampshade ring). Place the doily in the bowl of paste and move it around to get it well coated.

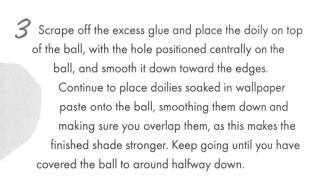

3 Scrape off the excess glue and place the doily on top of the ball, with the hole positioned centrally on the ball, and smooth it down toward the edges. Continue to place doilies soaked in wallpaper paste onto the ball, smoothing them down and making sure you overlap them, as this makes the finished shade stronger. Keep going until you have covered the ball to around halfway down.

4 Leave the ball in the box in a warm dry place such as an airing cupboard to dry—at least overnight. When it is dry it should be hard when tapped with your fingernail. Mix up some more wallpaper paste and, using a paintbrush, apply another layer all over the doilies. Put it back in the airing cupboard to dry overnight and check it again the next day. You can repeat this step as many times as necessary, although one additional coat should be enough.

5 When your lampshade is sufficiently solid, pull out the valve on the ball and wait until it has deflated enough for you to be able to run your hand under the doilies to release them from the ball.

6 Apply strong white glue around the edge of the hole on the inside and press the lampshade ring on to it. Weight it down with something heavy such as a plate and a storage jar until the glue is dry and the ring is fixed securely.

why not

Use a large bowl or flowerpot
as a mold to get a different
shaped shade.

Use vintage fabric remnants and fabric stiffener to make this unusual spherical shade. The ball is made from eight panels, four of which are made from two pieces of fabric and four of which are made from three pieces of fabric.

Patchwork ball

1 Start by making the templates for your fabric pieces. Use a tape measure to find out the circumference of the beach ball and make a note of it. Take another measurement, this time 2 in. (5 cm) above the original measurement and then again 2 in. (5 cm) above that.

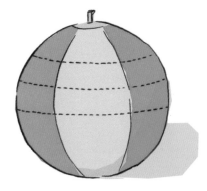

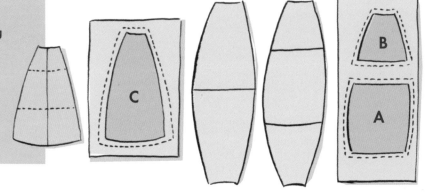

2 Divide all three measurements by eight and draw a template, tapering to 1¼ in. (3 cm) wide at the top. Trace round this shape, adding a ¼ in. (6 mm) border all round. This is template C. Take the original template and double it to create a panel-shaped template. Trace round this shape and then cut it into three parts. Add a ¼ in. (6 mm) border to the top and center pieces—these are templates B and A. You should now have three templates—A, B, and C.

why not

Recycle old dish towels, hankies, and clothing for your fabric patches.

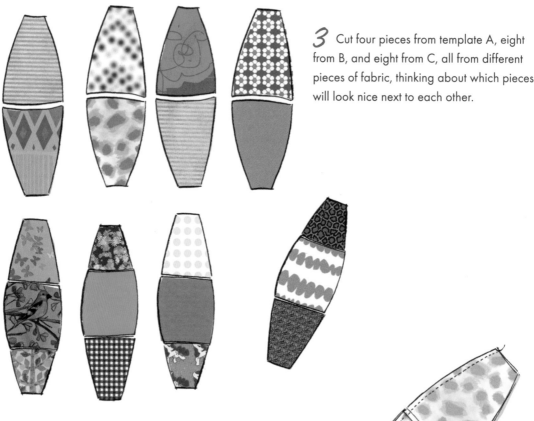

3 Cut four pieces from template A, eight from B, and eight from C, all from different pieces of fabric, thinking about which pieces will look nice next to each other.

4 With right sides together, stitch the pieces together to make eight panels, then trim seam allowances to ⅛ in. (3mm) and press to one side. When you have made up all eight panels, stitch them to each other, right sides together, in a row, alternating three-piece and two-piece panels.

5 Measure the circumference of the ring on your lampshade fitting and trim the top edge of your fabric panels so that the total width is ¾ in. (2 cm) less than the circumference of the ring. Trim the bottom edge so it is about 1¼ in. (3 cm) longer than the top edge. Bind both the top and bottom edges with bias binding tape.

6 Test the size by wrapping the fabric panel strip round the beach ball, and make any necessary adjustments to the seams. Trim the seams and press all the seams to the same side. When it fits smoothly over the ball, stitch the first panel to the eighth and trim the seam allowance. If you have a ham or sleeve board, press the seam to the same side as the others.

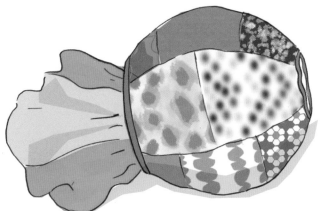

7 Partially deflate the beach ball so it fits through the larger hole and, with the valve at the smaller hole, blow it up so it fills out the fabric. The fabric should be taut, with no wrinkles. Thread a length of string through the loop in the valve and hang the ball up somewhere it can hang freely, for example from a shower curtain rail.

8 Use a paintbrush to apply a coat of fabric stiffener all over the patchwork ball. Leave to dry for a couple of hours before adding a second coat and leave for another couple of hours or overnight. Your fabric ball should be hard when tapped with your fingernail. If not, apply another coat of stiffener and leave to dry.

9 Deflate the beach ball and remove it through the large hole. Apply strong glue around the inside edge of the top (smaller) hole and stick the lampshade fitting to it by simply pressing it down.

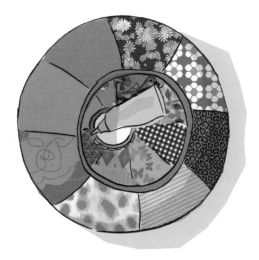

Chapter 3

PAPER, CARD, AND WOOD

It's amazing what you can do with a sheet of wallpaper or giftwrap, a collection of old hardback books, or some vintage hinged rulers. Or why not try making a shade from papier mâché?

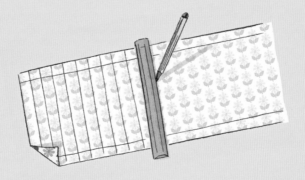

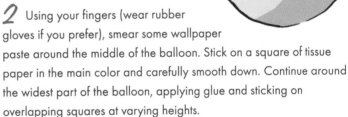

Papier mâché is really fun and easy to do and using a balloon for the basic shape gives this shade a lovely, retro feel—straight out of the 1970s! Using colored tissue paper means you can tie this lampshade in to your existing color scheme.

Papier mâché dome

You will need

Wallpaper paste

Bucket

Tissue paper in two colors, cut into squares of approximately 2 in. (5 cm)

Balloon

Approximately 80 in. (2 m) string

Rubber gloves (optional)

Top ring with gimbal fitting, taken from an old cone-shaped lampshade

Pencil

Scissors

Tape measure

Strong white glue

LED or low-wattage bulb

1 Make up a small amount of wallpaper paste in a bucket, following the manufacturer's instructions. Place your tissue paper squares in two separate bowls. Blow up your balloon, tie the end, and using a length of string, hang it from the ceiling so that the balloon is just lower than face height. A shower rail in the bathroom is ideal for this.

2 Using your fingers (wear rubber gloves if you prefer), smear some wallpaper paste around the middle of the balloon. Stick on a square of tissue paper in the main color and carefully smooth down. Continue around the widest part of the balloon, applying glue and sticking on overlapping squares at varying heights.

3 Moving upward toward the knot in the balloon, stick on more rows of squares in the same color in the same way, overlapping squares as you go. Repeat until you reach the knot.

4 Apply about three rows of squares in the second color around the bottom part of the balloon, overlapping some with the first row of the main color. Remember to leave the bottom part of the balloon uncovered. Untie the balloon and carefully hang it somewhere warm, such as the airing cupboard, to dry for a few hours or overnight.

5 Rehang the balloon in the bathroom and repeat steps 2–4 three or four more times, adding the occasional square in the second color towards the top, and vice versa.

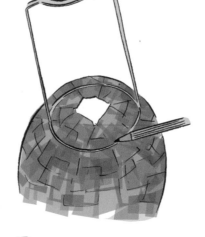

6 Leave to dry for a final time and the papier mâché layers should be hard to the touch. Untie and, with a needle, pop the balloon (this bit is very satisfying!) It should come away easily from the inside of the lampshade shell.

7 Place the top ring of the light fitting centrally over the small hole where the knot was and, using a pencil, draw onto the papier mâché round the inside of the ring.

8 Carefully cut round the line, just above your pencil line, so that you are making a hole that is just smaller than the ring of the light fitting.

9 Using a tape measure and pencil, measure 10 in. (25 cm), or whatever your required length, down to the bottom from the hole you cut in the top. Mark with a pencil all around the bottom so your pencil marks are a few inches (centimetres) apart. Carefully cut around this line, keeping it as straight as possible.

10 Apply glue around the hole inside the shade and press the light fitting on. Leave for at least an hour, weighted down with a book if possible.

why not?

If you are doing this project with kids, use flour and water instead of wallpaper paste because it is chemical-free.

Hunting through old secondhand stores can result in some really interesting finds—here a collection of old hinged rulers has been transformed into a real talking point. The shade looks just as good with the light off as it does on.

Vintage rulers

You will need

10–20 vintage hinged yard-sticks and rulers, depending on the size of your ring

Tape measure

Pencil

Hacksaw

Sandpaper

Drill with ¹⁄₁₆ in. (2 mm) bit

Pair of drum lampshade rings

Garden wire

1 Using a tape measure, mark out 8 in. (20 cm) sections on your yardsticks with a pencil, avoiding any brass hinges etc. Use a hacksaw to cut them to this length as neatly as possible, making sure they are all the same length. Sand the ends smooth with sandpaper.

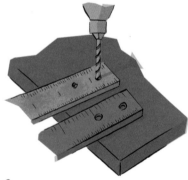

2 Mark a dot in the center, ³⁄₈ in. (1 cm) in from each end of each ruler, and another dot ³⁄₈ in. (1 cm) along from that. Use the drill to drill small holes where you have marked.

3 Measure the circumference of one of your lampshade rings and take a length of garden wire that is about three times this measurement. Thread the wire through the top hole in your first ruler, from back to front, then through the second hole, from front to back. Twist it back round itself, twist once around the ring and repeat with the next ruler.

why not?

Use different-colored wire for
a cool contrast effect.

4 When you have gone right round the
ring, making sure that the rulers are evenly
spaced, twist the two ends of wire together
to secure. Trim the ends and tuck the twist up
under the ring to hide. Repeat step 3 with
the other ring and the holes at the other
ends of the rulers.

This is so simple to make—and fun too. I used 1970s French floral wallpaper but any good-quality wallpaper would do. The finished shade is amazingly rigid and strong for something made out of paper.

Pleated wallpaper

You will need

80 in. (2 m) vintage wallpaper

Pair of cone lampshade rings—5 in. (12 cm) top ring with a hinged gimbal fitting and 12 in. (30 cm) lower ring

Glue stick

Sewing machine

Matching sewing thread

Ruler and pencil

Single hole punch

Scissors

1 Cut a piece of wallpaper at least twice the circumference of the bottom ring (in this case 80 in./2m) and 8 in. (20 cm) high. If your wallpaper has a design that runs vertically like the one shown, you will need to cut several pieces that are 8 in. (20 cm) high and join them at the sides to make one long piece. To do this, overlap two pieces slightly, use a glue stick to stick together and then zigzag stitch along the seam using a sewing machine.

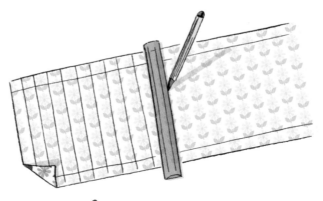

why not

Use offcuts of wallpaper left over from home decorating projects—or stick together sheets of good-quality giftwrap.

2 On the reverse of the paper, measure and mark in light pencil two lines, ¾ in. (2 cm) from each long edge. Then lightly mark lines ¾ in. (2 cm) apart across the width of the paper.

3 Fold the paper into a concertina along these lines, using the edge of a table and/or a ruler to help you get nice sharp folds.

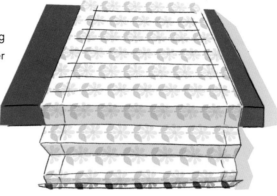

4 Using your hole punch, make holes halfway across each fold of the concertina, positioning them on the pencil line along the top edge. Missing out the first "fold," punch through both layers of the next "fold" and work all the way across, leaving one "fold" unpunched at the other end. Repeat along the bottom edge.

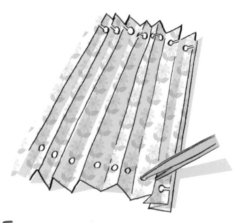

5 Use scissors to make snips along the pencil line from each outward fold to each hole. Repeat along the other long edge. Attach the two short ends together with glue and machine stitch as before. Punch holes in this overlap and snip as before.

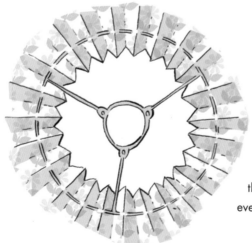

6 Press both lampshade rings through the slits so they sit in the holes, making sure that the pleats are evenly distributed either side of the gimbal at the top.

You can sometimes judge a book by its cover—when the cover is better than the contents. Use unwanted secondhand hardback books to make this modernist-style lampshade.

Hardback books

1 Remove any dust jackets from the books and use a pencil and ruler to mark our your chosen shapes. You need to make four squares made up of two colors and each finished square should be 8 x 8 in. (20 x 20 cm). Use the scalpel and cutting mat to cut out the shapes.

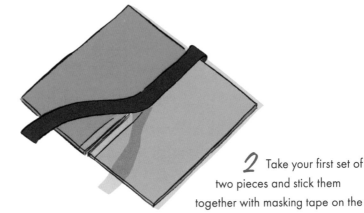

2 Take your first set of two pieces and stick them together with masking tape on the back. Stick double-stick tape down each side of the join on the front and then wrap it round to the back at the ends. Press on a length of grosgrain ribbon, folding it over the edges onto the back. Repeat on all four squares.

3 Lay the squares out in a row and stick double-stick tape down each vertical edge, either side of where the squares will join together. Remove the backing tape.

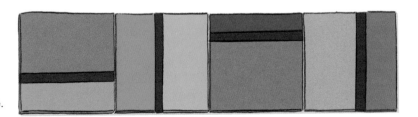

why not

Use book covers with typography or patterns, or use the inside of the covers—some have lovely endpapers.

4 Join the four squares together in a row by pressing the green ribbon onto the tape, making sure that the pieces can still bend at a right angle.

5 Stick double-stick tape along both long edges, front and back, and apply the gold braid, folding it over to the back and pressing to secure.

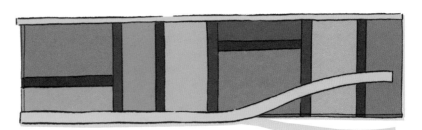

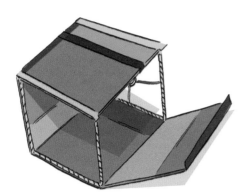

6 Peel off the backing from the PVC and stick it to the back of your cardboard squares. You should have a ¾ in. (2 cm) overlap at one end—fold this up to a right angle. Apply double-stick tape to the outside of both lampshade rings and, starting at the end without the overlap, "roll" them along the edges of the PVC, aligning the corners with the joins between the squares. When you get to the end, continue "rolling" onto the overlap and press down to stick.

7 Finish off this final corner with another length of green ribbon, attached as before with double-stick tape. Fold the ends over and tuck them around the lampshade rings at the top and bottom.

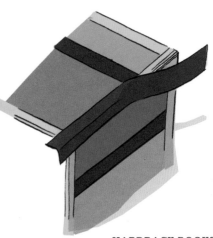

why not

Cover an old existing drum-shaped lampshade, starting at step 2. It doesn't matter if it's wider—you will just need a larger piece of paper.

This Oriental-looking shade can be used on a table or ceiling light, or on a standard lamp, depending where you place the fringe.

Paper lantern

1 Referring to the instructions for the Drum Lampshade on pages 14–17, make a drum shade 8 in. (20) cm high in your pale colored fabric.

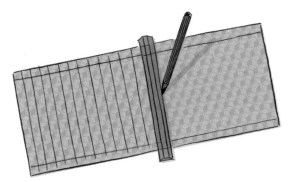

2 Cut a piece of patterned paper that is the length of the circumference of the lampshade rings, plus ⅜ in. (1 cm), and 10 in. (25 cm) wide. On the wrong side of the paper, mark a line ¾ in. (2 cm) away from each long edge. Then working across the width of the paper, mark lines 1¼ in. (3 cm) apart.

3 Fold the paper in half, long edge to long edge and with right sides together. Cut along the short lines through both layers of paper, starting at the fold and going up to the line ¾ in. (2 cm) from the edge. Open out the paper and refold it across the same fold, this time wrong sides together.

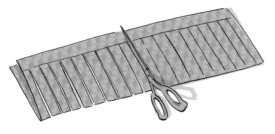

4 Stick double-stick tape to the wrong side of one long edge of the paper, as close to the edge as possible. Peel off the backing and, starting at the join, stick the paper to the very edge of the lampshade.

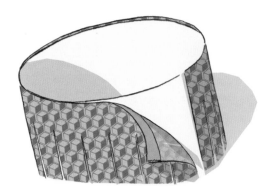

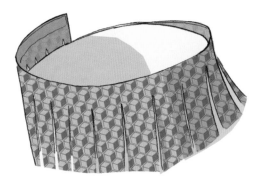

5 Carefully stick more tape along the lower edge of the paper and stick to the bottom of the lampshade in the same way.

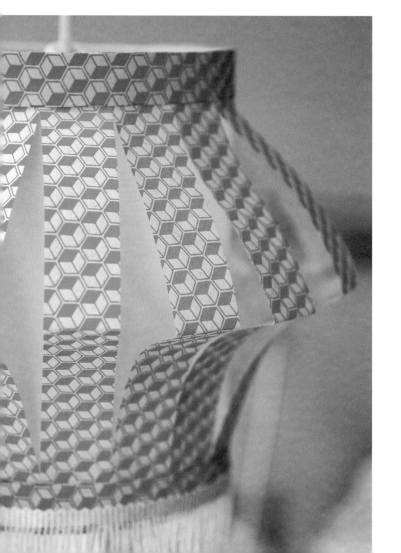

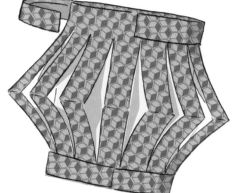

6 Cut two more strips of paper, each ¾ in. (2 cm) wide and long enough to go round the circumference of the lampshade with a ⅜ in. (1 cm) overlap. Stick them to the top and bottom edges of the lampshade with double-stick tape, very slightly overlapping the edge of the paper. If possible apply them so that the pattern runs in the opposite direction.

7 Apply a final length of double-stick tape to the bottom edge of the shade and stick on the fringe trim.

Older children will love making these paper cube lights and hanging them in their bedroom. Make sure you use LED fairy lights as they give off much less heat.

Origami fairy lanterns

1 Cut a 6 in. (15 cm) square from a piece of cardboard and use it as a template to cut out 40 squares of paper.

why not

Use children's drawings, origami paper, an old calendar, a map, or giftwrap to make your lanterns.

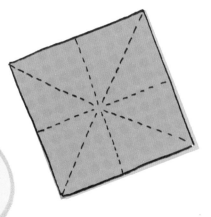

2 Take your first square and fold in half with right sides together. Open out the paper, turn it 90 degrees and repeat. Now turn the paper over and fold it diagonally, this time with wrong sides together. Turn 90 degrees and fold diagonally again.

3 Look for the triangle in the creases and push the sides in with your fingers. Press down to make a folded triangle. Fold the corner on the left hand side (top layer only) up to the middle. Do the same on the right hand side. Turn the whole thing over and do the same on the other side. Your paper is now a little square with a line across the middle.

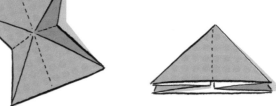

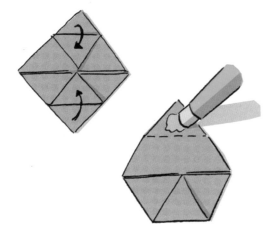

4 Lift one of the sides up and fold the point to the middle; fold the opposite side the same way. Now turn over and do the other side. Place a little glue under the two flaps, weigh down for a few minutes under a heavy book while you get on with making some more cubes.

5 Remove from under the book. On the right-hand side you will see two loose flaps. Fold, aligning outer edges, and push them into the little pockets. Turn over to do both sides. Fold the side out a little and blow hard into the little hole you see on the bottom.

6 Continue until you have made 40 cubes, or however many fairy lights are on your string. Once you have inflated all the cubes by blowing into them, push a fairy light bulb through each hole. Apply small strips of clear tape either side of any holes that are too large so that the bulbs stay in.

Chapter 4
METAL

Make stunning shades from everyday objects such as cookie tins, aluminum foil, old keys—even recycled tin cans.

These are so simple to make and are secured with elastic bands, which also add a splash of color. Metal sweet molds can be found online—try looking for vintage ones on online auction websites. Make sure you use LED fairy lights as you cannot use lights that give off any heat.

Sweet mold fairy lights

1 Take your first sweet mold and position upside down on a stable surface. Use the drill to make a hole in the center of the base of the mold. Take care—you may find it easier to make a small dent in the mold first by knocking a nail with a hammer where you want the hole, so the drill doesn't slip.

2 When you have made holes in all 40 molds, simply push an LED light bulb through the hole in the first mold.

3 To stop the bulb slipping out, secure each bulb by wrapping an elastic band around the cable just below the bulb inside the sweet mold shade. Alternate the shapes and sizes of the sweet molds and colors of rubber bands as you progress along the string.

why not

Give new metal molds a worn look by first soaking them in bleach and vinegar—they should rust slightly as they dry.

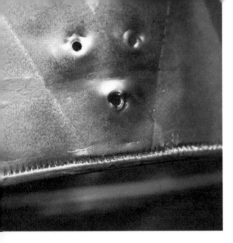

Transform a large tin can into a striking metallic art deco-effect lampshade. The holes in the tin create a wonderful effect when the light is switched on.

Art Deco punched tin

1 Use a can opener to remove the lid of the can (keep the base on for now as it helps the can retain its shape when you drill holes in it). Pour out the contents, wash out, and, if necessary, soak to remove the label and scrape off any glue.

You will need

Large tin can, approximately 8 in. (20 cm) tall

Large, heavy-duty "butterfly" can opener (one that cuts downward, leaving the can intact rather than the lid)

Tape measure

Permanent marker pen

Drill with various sized bits

Masking tape

Gold and silver spray paint

Craft knife

Lampshade ring with gimbal, the same diameter as the tin (in this case 6½ in./16 cm)

Strong glue

Butterfly clips

2 With a tape measure, measure the circumference of the can so you can work out your design. My can measured 19½ in. (49 cm) round, so I started by marking zigzags 2¾ in. (7 cm) apart in small dots, using the tape measure and a permanent marker pen. Mark further designs with more dots.

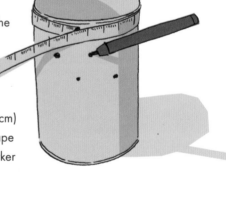

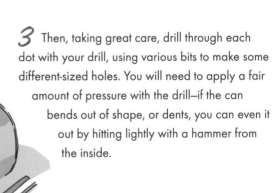

3 Then, taking great care, drill through each dot with your drill, using various bits to make some different-sized holes. You will need to apply a fair amount of pressure with the drill—if the can bends out of shape, or dents, you can even it out by hitting lightly with a hammer from the inside.

4 Cover the holes on the inside with masking tape. Spread out an old sheet or some other covering for protection in a well-ventilated area indoors. Place your tin base-down on a pedestal such as a smaller tin. Shake the gold spray paint well before using and then spray the outside of the tin with it, from a distance of about 24 in. (60 cm). Carefully move the tin round as you go, taking care not to touch the wet paint. Leave to dry for a few hours or overnight if time allows.

5 When the gold paint is fully dry, stick masking tape to the outside of the can, following the zigzag shape made by the holes and adding triangle shapes to the bottom edge. Press the tape down well and trim away any excess tape around the top and bottom of the can with a craft knife.

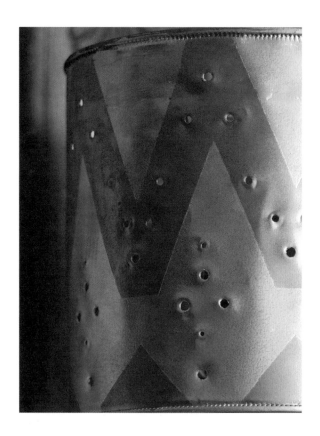

6 Spray the outside of the can with silver spray paint as in step 4. Leave to dry overnight and then carefully remove all masking tape. Use the tin opener to remove the base, taking care not to scratch the metallic paint.

7 Using strong glue, stick the lampshade ring to the inside of your can at the bottom. Use butterfly clips to hold the ring in place while the glue dries. If the ring is exactly the same size, you may find that the ring fits snugly and stays fixed without any glue.

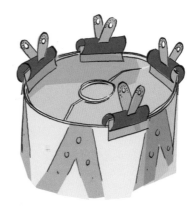

why not

If your keys are rusty, soak them in white vinegar overnight and then scrub them with a brush. You could also spray them with metallic spray paint.

Old-fashioned keys often look lovely and can be bought fairly cheaply. Hung from a lampshade ring with various colored ribbons, they move in a breeze and sometimes make a "dinging" sound when they knock together.

Hanging keys

You will need

About 20 old keys in various shapes and sizes

Two or three small padlocks

Lengths of braid, ribbon, and ricrac in assorted colors

A 7 in. (18 cm) diameter shade carrier or slip uno fitter (the gimbal has long arms that extend to the top ring)

1 Match each key with a piece of ribbon or trim of a corresponding thickness and weight.

2 Fold each piece of ribbon in half and thread it double through the hole in the key or padlock. Thread the ends through the loop and pull to make a knot.

3 Decide how high or low you want each key to hang and trim the ribbon accordingly. Press under ¼ in. (6 mm) at each end of the ribbon or trim, and, with the ribbon wrapped around the shade carrier, pin then neatly stitch the ends together.

4 Hang the remainder of the keys and padlocks in the same way, arranging them at various heights.

This takes a steady hand but the finished result looks wonderful with the light shining through—every cloud has a silver lining!

Metal clouds

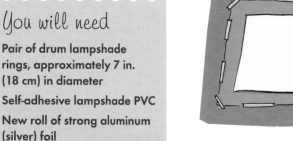

You will need

Pair of drum lampshade rings, approximately 7 in. (18 cm) in diameter

Self-adhesive lampshade PVC

New roll of strong aluminum (silver) foil

Transparent adhesive tape

Template on page 125

Cardboard for template

Sharp pencil

Pair of nail scissors (with a curved blade)

Double-stick lampshade tape, ¼ in. (6 mm) wide

Ruler, scalpel, and cutting mat

1 Decide how tall you want your lampshade to be and measure the circumference of your lampshade rings. Following the instructions for the Drum Lampshade on pages 14–17, cut a piece of PVC to the correct size. Working from a new roll, unroll a piece of foil that is longer than the PVC. Smooth it out and stick it securely to your work surface at all four corners and around all the edges with tape, making sure it is smooth and taut.

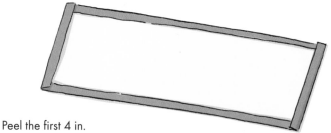

2 Peel the first 4 in. (10 cm) of backing from the PVC and carefully stick it centrally on the foil, then pull away the backing, little by little with your right hand while smoothing down with your left (or vice versa). Work slowly and take great care to smooth out as many bubbles and creases as you can. Trim the foil to about ⅜ in. (1 cm) all around and then roughly tuck the foil border around the edges of the PVC.

3 Transfer the template on page 125 onto a piece of thin cardboard. Decide where you want to position your clouds and then use a sharp pencil to draw around the template on the foil, taking care to leave the central bar intact.

4 Using the scalpel, cutting mat and ruler, cut along the straight bottom edge of the clouds, going right through the foil and PVC but leaving the central bar attached.

why not

Simplify this project by using metallic paper, or by cutting out shapes with straight edges—remembering to leave them attached by a central bar.

5 Then use the nail scissors to carefully cut around the curved edges of the clouds.

6 Unfold the foil border from the edges of the PVC and then cut away all the border from one short edge, leaving it flush with the edge of the PVC. Stick double-stick tape along the other short edge of the PVC, peel off the backing, and fold the foil border over onto it. Press down and then stick another piece of tape right on the edge of this foil overlap, leaving the backing on.

7 Apply double-sided tape to the outside of the rings and, following the instructions for Drum Lampshade on pages 14–17, roll them along the edges of the PVC.

8 To finish, use your fingertips to tuck the excess foil at the top and bottom around the rings.

Old tins are often so lovely to look at but if they've gone a little rusty or scratched, here is a wonderful new way to display them.

Vintage cookie tin chandelier

You will need

Three vintage cookie or candy tins in different sizes

Large, heavy-duty "butterfly" can opener (one that cuts downward, leaving the can intact rather than the lid)

Approximate 40 in. (1 m) ribbon

Double-stick lampshade tape, ¼ in. (6 mm) wide

Tape measure

Marker pen

80 in. (2 m) chain from a DIY store, with links approximately ⅜ in. (1 cm) in diameter

Fifteen large ¾ in. (2 cm) jump rings

Drill with ⅛ in. (3 mm) metal bit

Two pairs of pliers

Metal ring for hanging, 1¼ in. (3 cm) in diameter

1 Remove the lids from the cookie tins and discard (or save them for another project). Using a can opener, carefully cut the bases off the tins. Cover any raw or sharp edges inside the tin with ribbon, using double-stick tape.

2 Use a tape measure to measure the circumference of the largest tin. Divide the measurement by three and, with a marker pen, mark three dots this distance apart on the inside of the tin, ⅜ in. (1 cm) from the top edge. Mark three more matching dots ⅜ in. (1 cm) from the bottom edge. Measure and mark the medium-sized tin in the same way. Do the same with the smallest tin but mark the three dots around its top edge only. Use the drill to drill holes through the tins where you have marked.

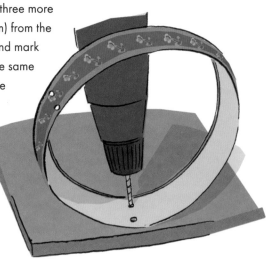

why not

Add as many tins as you like—you
could also use square ones.

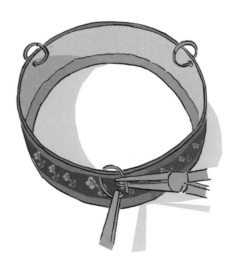

3 Using two pairs of pliers, open a jump ring by twisting the ends sideways. You need to open it wide enough to get it through a hole in the tin, and then close it up by twisting the ends back together again with the pliers. Repeat for all the holes in all three tins.

4 Take the chain and, using pliers to open up the links, make six sets of two links. Attach these to the three jump rings at the bottom edge of the large tin and the three jump rings at the bottom of the medium-sized tin. Close each link firmly with the pliers.

5 Attach the chains D to G, E to H, and F to I. Then attach chains J to M, K to N, and L to O. Make three 18 in. (45 cm) lengths of chain (make them longer or shorter depending on the height of your ceiling light) and attach one each to jump rings A, B and C. Attach the other ends of the three long chains to the 1¼ in. (3 cm) metal ring to hang from a chandelier ceiling fitting.

Chapter 5
ODDS AND ENDS

The beauty of upcycling comes into its own in this chapter as a range of items, from old photographic slides to vintage sewing items, are turned into lovely lampshades.

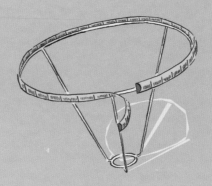

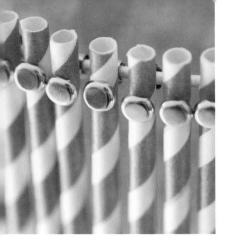

A simple, fun lampshade made out of old-fashioned striped drinking straws and brass paper fasteners.

Striped straws

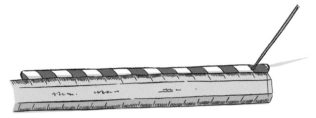

1 Using a thick needle, make a hole in each straw ⅜ in. (1 cm) from the end, going right the way through and out the other side.

2 Take a brass brad (paper fastener) and, with the "legs" going horizontally across the width of the straw and the longer "leg" on top, poke it through the hole. Continue until you have stuck brads through as many straws as you think you'll need.

3 Position your lampshade ring on a lamp base and then splay out the legs of one of the brads.

4 Start fixing the straws to the lampshade ring. Line the straw up on the outside of the ring and fold the lower "leg" of the brad up around the ring, giving it a squeeze with the pliers. Fold the upper "leg" down over the first one and around the ring, and squeeze with the pliers again. Continue until your lampshade ring is covered in straws, finishing off by neatening any brads that are folded over unevenly.

why not

Use pastel-colored or white plastic straws instead.

A fun way to display family pictures from days gone by—or find old slides in junk or thrift stores to make this truly original piece.

Photographic slides

You will need

Lampshade ring with a slip uno fitter (the gimbal has long arms that extend to the top ring)

Tape measure

Vintage photographic slides—You will need about 30 for a 6 in. (16 cm) diameter ring

Drill with ¹⁄₁₆ in. (2 mm) bit

Small jewelry pliers

Jump rings

LED or low-wattage bulb

1 Measure the circumference of your ring and the width of one slide (most are 2 in./5 cm) to work out how many you will need to go round the ring, allowing for a small gap between each one, about ¼ in. (5 mm). You may need to use a particular size of jump ring depending on how the slides fit and what size the gaps need to be.

2 Arrange your slides in three rows, so that landscape and portrait slides are randomly spaced, as well as any with different logos. Keep the image upright.

3 Make a template from a spare slide. Measure halfway across and a little way in from the edge and mark and drill a hole. Measure again to check the hole is still in the center and then place it on top of a pile of three slides. Drill through all three slides, turning the template to make holes on all four edges—but remember, the slides on the bottom row don't need holes on their lower edges.

4 Use the pliers to open the jump rings and start attaching the slides together through the holes, in vertical rows of three.

5 Now attach two rows of three slides together with three more jump rings. Add jump rings to the two slides at the top. Repeat with the rest of the slides. Place the lampshade ring on your lamp base and start hanging the slides, in groups of six slides. Repeat until all the slides are hanging from the ring and then use more jump rings to attach each group of six to its neighbor.

6 Finally, make adjustments by opening or closing any jump rings to correct any slides that are hanging unevenly.

why not

Paint the cardboard borders of the slides all one color to cover any logos and make them all uniform.

Washi is a type of decorative paper tape that originated in Japan. It can be made from bamboo, hemp, rice, and wheat and comes in every color and pattern imaginable! This is so simple as the strips of washi tape can easily be removed and repositioned.

Washi tape

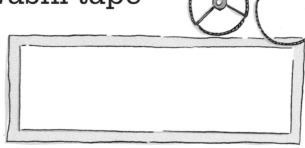

1 Referring to the instructions for the Drum Lampshade on pages 14–17, cut a piece of PVC to the size required for the size of your lampshade rings. Apply double-stick tape to both rings (but leave the backing tape on for now); set aside. Cut a piece of vinyl that is about ¾ in. (2 cm) larger than the PVC all around.

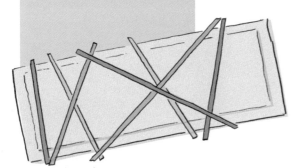

2 Start sticking strips of washi tape randomly across the shiny side of the vinyl, leaving about ¾ in. (2 cm) of extra tape overlapping the edge of the vinyl. Space the different colored tape randomly but evenly in all directions.

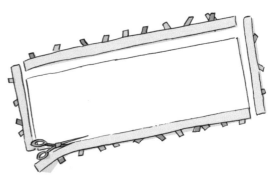

3 When you are happy with your design, position your piece of PVC on the wrong side of the vinyl, following the instructions for the Drum Lampshade on pages 14–17. Trim away any excess vinyl from the edges so it is completely flush with the PVC.

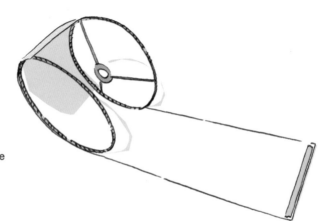

4 Stick a couple of pieces of double-stick tape next to each other right at one short edge of the PVC—don't peel off the backing just yet. Peel the backing tape off the lampshade rings and roll the two rings along the edges of the PVC. Peel away the backing from the tape on the end of the PVC and press firmly to stick down along the overlap.

why not
Make a plain vinyl shade and decorate it with stickers instead of tape.

If you like rummaging in craft shops and thrift stores, you'll love this bell shade adorned with a collection of crafty accessories.

Stitcher's delight

1 If necessary, clean and remove any flaking paint from your frame, then tightly bind it with wool, using a different color for the top and bottom ring and each vertical strut.

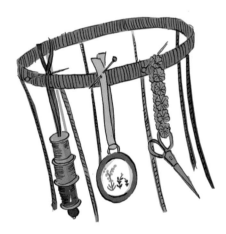

2 Match each item to be hung with a colored ribbon, string, or kilt pin and pin them all around the top ring of the frame at various heights.

3 When you are happy with the arrangement, secure each ribbon or string with a few neat hand stitches. Remove any kilt pins for now.

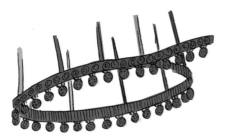

4 Pin and hand stitch the ricrac around the top ring, Reattach any kilt pins. Then pin and hand stitch the pompom trim to the edge of the bottom ring.

why not

Use sewing and knitting items handed down from your mom, aunt, or grandma—this is a lovely way of displaying items with sentimental value that you don't want to use.

Get a macramé-like effect without all the complicated knotting with this brightly colored hanging shade, which would look great in a conservatory.

Bead chandelier

1 Cut six lengths of piping cord, each 60 in. (150 cm), and pass them all through the small metal ring so that the 12 ends are hanging level.

2 Hang the ring from a hook or tie it onto something at eye level. Tie a whip knot just under the ring and then snip off the two loose ends close to the knot.

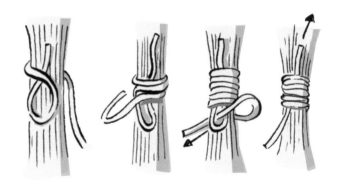

3 Measure 14 in. (35 cm) down from the knot at the top (or whatever the distance that your light bulb hangs from the ceiling) and mark each cord at this point by sticking a pin right through it. Starting tying the cords all round the larger ring with double knots, exactly where the marker pins are. Make sure the cords don't cross over or get tangled and remove the pins as you go. It may be easier to have someone help you by holding the top ring.

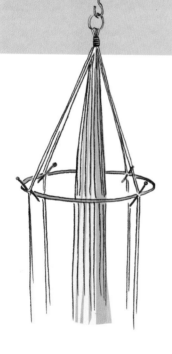

why not

Use the inside of wooden or plastic
embroidery hoops as the rings.

4 Remove from the hook and hold up to make sure the ring is hanging level; adjust the knots if necessary.

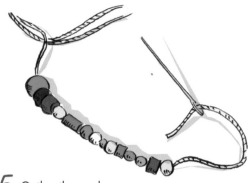

5 Gather the cord ends in a bunch and turn the whole thing over, laying it down on a flat surface. Using a bodkin, thread 7 in. (18 cm) of beads onto the first cord, starting with the larger beads and finishing with smaller ones. Knot the end loosely to secure while you repeat on the other 11 cords.

6 With double knots, tie all 12 cords to the smaller ring where the rows of beads end. Hold the chandelier up to check it's level and even, and adjust any of the knots if necessary. Trim the ends to ¾ in. (2 cm).

7 Check that the bead strings are evenly spaced around the rings and then take a long piece of cord and use it to bind the large center and bottom rings. Wind the cord tightly and neatly around, covering the loose ends on the bottom ring. Secure the end with a knot and sew in with the bodkin before cutting off.

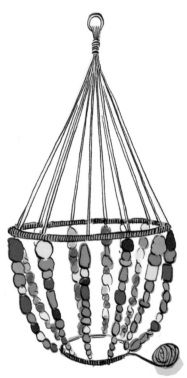

Templates and charts

Applique skyline

page 32

enlarge to 200 percent

Cross stitch campsite

page 54

enlarge to 150 percent

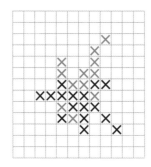

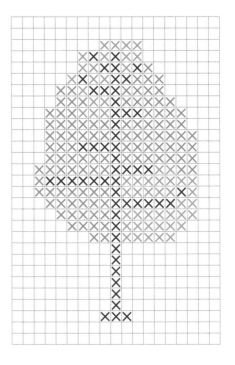

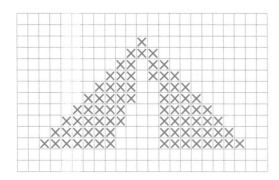

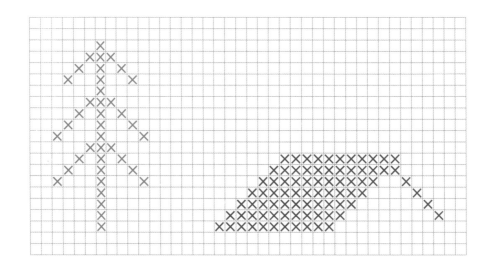

Birdhouse

page 56

enlarge to 150 percent

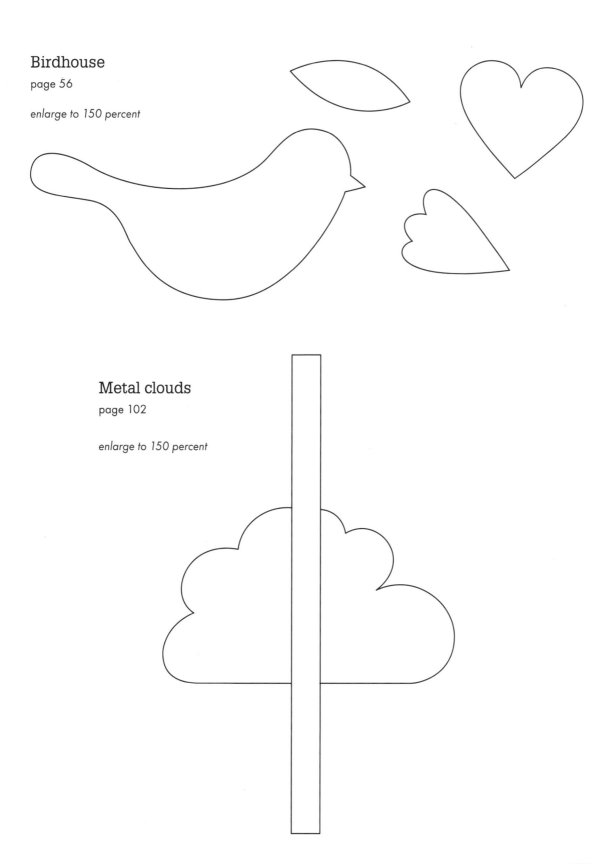

Metal clouds

page 102

enlarge to 150 percent

Suppliers and useful addresses

UK

THE CLOTH HOUSE
47 Berwick Street
London, W1F 8SJ
+44 (0)20 7437 5155
www.clothhouse.com
Innovative fabrics from around the world

DONNA FLOWER
www.donnaflower.com
Online store specializing in antique, vintage and retro fabrics

FRED ALDOUS
www.fredaldous.co.uk
Suppliers of specialist lampshade-making materials

LIBERTY
Regent Street
London, W1B 5AH
+44 (0)20 7734 1234
www.liberty.co.uk
Furnishing fabrics and haberdashery

MACCULLOCH AND WALLIS
25–26 Dering Street
London, W1S 1AT
+44 (0)20 7629 0311
www.macculloch-wallis.co.uk
Fabrics, haberdashery, and trimmings

M IS FOR MAKE
www.misformake.co.uk
Online fabric shop

NEEDCRAFT
www.needcraft.co.uk
Suppliers of specialist lampshade-making materials

SPINSTER'S EMPORIUM
www.spinstersemporium.co.uk
Vintage fabrics, haberdashery, and other craft materials

WAYWARD
68 Norman Road
St. Leonards On Sea
East Sussex
TN38 0EJ
+44 (0)7815 013337
www.wayward.co
Vintage fabrics and haberdashery

US

BROOKLYN GENERAL STORE
128 Union Street
Brooklyn
NY 11231
718 237-7753
www.brooklyngeneral.com
Yarn, fabric, notions and more

GREYS FABRIC AND NOTIONS
450 Harrison Avenue
63 Boston
MA 02118
617 338-4739
www.greysfabric.com
Boutique fabric shop

THE KNITTN KITTEN
7530 N.E. Glisan Street
Portland
Oregon 97213
503 255-3022
www.knittnkitten.com
Fabric and notions store

THE LAMP SHOP
www.lampshop.com
Suppliers of specialist lampshade-making materials

PINS AND NEEDLES
1045 Lexington Avenue,
2nd Floor
New York
NY 10021
212 535-6222
www.pinsandneedlesnyc.com
Sewing, fabric, and craft store

Other Places to Look

Online auction or market places such as ebay or Etsy.

CAR BOOT SALES (UK AND EU)
www.carbootsales.org
Search for local sales near you—I particularly like the Ford Airfield Car Boot Sale near Chichester, Sussex

FLEA MARKETS ACROSS AMERICA (US)
www.fleamarketsacrossamerica.com
Browse flea markets and fair by state

THE FREECYCLE NETWORK (WORLDWIDE)
www.freecycle.org

Index

Acknowledgments

Thanks to all those friends and family members who have taken an interest in my lampshades over the past three years, especially Sam for taking photos right at the start, Kim and Kim's friend Mary for the great fabric, Dad, Liz, Sarah, Lora and the ladies—and a very special thank you, a "chin chin" and a warm hug to Lauren. Thanks to Marisa for the chance to teach in the beautiful surroundings of the V&A; the *Prima* team past and present, with a special mention to Karen and Renée for the support, laughs and cups of tea, to Nina and Emma for letting me practice on them, and to anyone who has put on, or taken part in, one of my workshops and helped spread the word. Three cheers to Sigur Ros for the lampshade-making soundtrack and eternal gratitude to Natalie Lue for countless life lessons. Love always and thanks to Rich for everything.

I would also like to thank the Cico team for giving me the opportunity to do the book: Cindy Richards, Penny Craig and Sally Powell. Thanks to Isobel Gillan and Emma Mitchell—and to Clare Sayer and Michael Hill for all your hard work and patience.